How to Start, Run, and Grow a

Quick Service Fast Food Restaurant

Tips and Tricks from an Industry Veteran – Franchise or Non-Franchise

By

Robert Winfield

Copyrighted Material

Copyright © Autumn Leaf Publishing Press, 2020

Email: **Publisher@AutumnLeafPub@gmail.com**

All Rights Reserved.

Without limiting the rights under the copyright laws, no part of this publication may be reproduced, stored in or introduced into a retrieval system, or transmitted, in any form or by any means (electronic, mechanical, photocopying, recording or otherwise), without the prior written consent of the publisher of this book.

Autumn Leaf Publishing Press publishes its books and guides in a variety of electronic and print formats, Some content that appears in print may not be available in electronic format, and vice versa.

Autumn Leaf Publishers

Design & Illustration by Jordy Roberts

First Edition

Contents

Introduction 9

The Industry of Fast Food 24

    Fast Food Throughout History 25

    Modern Evolution of Fast Food 26

    A Cultural Phenomenon 30

    Global Perspective 34

    The Experience of Fast Food 37

    The Globalization of Food 39

Entrepreneurial Flair 42

    Positives 43

    Negatives 44

    Being Original 47

    Become an Expert 49

    Be Honest with Yourself 51

    Define Your Strengths 53

    Plan to Deal with Setbacks 54

Practicalities of Starting a Business 56

Register Your Company 57

Find Your Corner... 58

Start with Social Media.. 59

Location and Competition 60

Branding 63

    What's in a Name?.. 67

    Image is Everything.. 69

    Consistent Originality 70

The Business Plan 71

Dealing with the Bank.. 76

    Be Authentic 79

    Be Resilient... 80

    Alternatives to Bank Loans 82

Other Costs to Consider... 84

    Insurance 85

    Licensing... 87

    Equipment 89

Running the Business... 96

    Cleanliness Matters... 98

- Expanding the Business 103
  - Be Confident 106
  - The Road Map 108
    - Go Mobile 108
    - Sell Wholesale 109
    - Sell Franchise Rights 110
  - Future Trends 110
    - Home Delivery 111
    - Offer Healthier Options 112
    - Order Ahead/Mobile Ordering 113
- Points to Remember 115
- Part Two: Franchises 117
  - Franchises 118
  - Choices 120
  - Worth the Cost 122
- What a Franchise is 125
  - Big Names 128
  - Industry Innovation 129
- Money Matters 131

Contractual Matters 133

Franchise Starting Costs 135

    McDonald's 137

    Subway 139

    Wendy's 140

    Domino's Pizza 142

    Taco Bell 142

    Kentucky Fried Chicken 144

Other Profitable Ventures 145

    Wingstop 146

    Jersey Mike's Subs 146

    Krispy Kreme Donuts 147

    Firehouse Subs 149

    Dairy Queen 150

Less Expensive Franchises 152

    Champs Chicken 153

    Yum Yum Donuts 154

    Checkers/Rally's 155

    Baskin Robbins 156

- The Corporate Culture 158
  - The Real Cost to You 162
  - Business Partners 164
  - The Food Chain, So to Speak 166
  - A Note Regarding Contracts 168
- The Future of Franchises 170
  - Global Influence 171
  - Reaching a Broader Scope 173
  - Non-Food Franchises 174
    - Fit4Mom 174
    - Stratus Building Solutions 175
    - SuperGlass Windshield Repair 176
    - Dream Vacations 177
- CONCLUSION 180
- BIBLIOGRAPHY 183

This book is intended as a general guide to opening and running a fast food restaurant or taking on a franchise. Please note that the conditions, situations, and events contained herein may differ under the law in many countries around the world. Always take the advice of a good, knowledgeable lawyer or accountant in your region to get the best possible guidance on the risks and pitfalls of the venture ahead.

> *"Tough times never last, but tough people do."*
>
> Robert H Schuller – pastor, speaker, author

INTRODUCTION

Before we start, I have a confession to make. I am not an American citizen. I am a British citizen, English to be precise, with an awful plummy accent to match. So, I hope you won't hold that against me as we journey through the following pages.

Yet I can hear the cries now. What does a Brit know about fast food? After all, we Americans invented it!

Sorry, you didn't – but more of that later. In reality, the rest of the world did over the course of over 2000 years.

My journey began in the mid-1980s. I had tried a lot of things with not much success. I had a wife and a young child, and my only asset was a house that had made me a bit of money. You could say I was at a crossroads, very unsure of which path to take.

I had always liked cooking, probably a skill my mother introduced me to when I was a boy. We lived in the country miles from the nearest shop. Supermarkets and their big brothers were not even a blip on anyone's radar way back then. Neither of my parents drove, so we obviously did not have a car. A delivery van came on Monday and Thursday, and the local bus service ran on Wednesday, Friday, and Saturday. All in all, we were limited in choice.

My parents urged me to build a garden and plant things as they did, which meant that within a couple of years, we were pretty self-sufficient with seasonal vegetables. So, you have the raw ingredients. You then had to do something with them. Today's kitchen staples, such as the use of garlic, herbs, and spices, were virtually unknown, and our food was a pretty boring affair.

I was encouraged to turn the raw ingredients into something, to experiment, to get burned, to fail, to screw up, to throw away, but above all, to learn. A few years later, we took our first trip abroad, by rail from France to Spain, and boy, did that open my eyes. Not only were the sights amazing, but so were the accompanying smells.

A little exercise - close your eyes and take yourself back to your childhood. Of course, you can remember the people and places, but it is the smell of food that makes the jigsaw stick together. Your mother, your father, the heartbeat of the kitchen, and the taste of love made real!

It was not until a few years later, when we went to Italy, that I really started on a journey, one that has become a lifelong passion - Italian food. Arriving in Venice at 14 years of age, I found myself in a place I had never been before, yet I knew I really belonged.

I was allowed to roam the streets on my own, knowing where I wanted to go, what I wanted to see, and what I wanted to eat. I was immensely lucky to have liberal parents, especially my mother, who encouraged me to give free rein to the things that floated my boat. I love art, and Venice is full of it. I love architecture, and Venice is full of it. I love Venice because it is still one of the most beautiful cities in the world. I loved it all - smelly canals, damp hotel sheets, and the allure of the food.

From the fish market in Chioggia to the vegetable market across the Rialto Bridge, and the endless barges piled high that clog the side canal every day. They tried to sell you everything you may have ever wanted but didn't know you actually needed.

Above all, though, at the time, it was the "Nonnas," the pasta Grandmothers sitting in groups outside their open doors, trays on laps, rolling endless shapes and twirls of fresh pasta that intrigued me. They are now a rare sight, as the city's population has dwindled to fewer than 50K, all of whom are, in one way or another, involved in the tourist trade.

Seeing all this led me on a journey, not only to see places but to taste as many exotic things as I could. A few years later, I was in Czechoslovakia, 20 years before the wall fell. Likewise, I traveled to Russia and then Poland, each giving tastes I had never encountered before. I devoured the rest of Europe, Austria, Germany, France, Spain, and learned more.

I traveled across the United States, from San Francisco to the Baha, from the Baha to Las Vegas, from New Orleans to Washington, and then onto New York. I was fortunate to live for a while in the Carolinas, tasting the fresh produce of the Atlantic coast.

A few years later, I lived in Paris for 6 months, which gave me a handle on French cuisine, and then, a few years later, I crossed the top of the Sahara in a Land Rover. In the camel market at Nabul, thick Arabic coffee and the smell of the hookah pipe filled the air.

That was my culinary history. With that in mind, I made the choice to put the past behind me, sell the house, use the money to move 200 miles away from London, and reinvent myself as a pasta maker.

Plymouth is an old garrison town with one of the largest naval bases in the UK, completely remodeled by the Luftwaffe's operations in the early 1940s, when we were at war with one another. Since the character was knocked out of it, it was rebuilt as mile after mile of grey stone houses, each one looking exactly the same as the last.

In the city center, there was a huge, ill-advised, and certainly ill-thought-out shopping complex. Not exactly a mall, as no one had invented them yet. This shopping center has since been knocked down and replaced by a proper mall, but it was one ragtag mess of shops that had no idea how they actually complemented each other.

It was one of the horrible cement monstrosities thrown up in years of hasty reconstruction, only to be knocked down again when someone had a better idea.

It was there that I rented my first shop unit and brought fresh pasta to the West Country of England. Now, what is funny about that is that if you then said "pasta" to someone from the region, they would assume you were saying "pasty," a food the region is synonymous with. For those unaware, it was the day's takeaway staple.

The pasty was invented in the 18th Century by housewives for their husbands who worked in the tin and arsenic mines, which were the main employers at the time. It was a large, enclosed, half-circle, baked pastry, filled with diced potatoes, vegetables, and meat. On the top side was a particularly thick crust, meant to be held whilst eating and then discarded once finished. Carry on eating, of course, and whatever residue was left on the surface would eventually kill you, necessitating your bereaved wife to look for another husband. Hence, the Cornish Pasty was invented.

Everyone thought I was mad. "Pasties, boy, not pasta. Never catch on. No, not for us," was the general consensus. Still, I persisted, did my research, and chose an empty spot in a fairly central area with a lot of passing customers from the shopping center. I then built a fully fitted kitchen over a ceramic-tiled floor in the empty unit. I bought some pasta-making machines from a London vendor; likewise, utensils and crockery, fridges, and various cookers.

I painted the walls in the colors of the Italian flag – red, green, and white. I decided I would have minimal space for eating. I wanted people to buy and leave, certainly not hang about. I placed a counter around the window that looked out onto the walkway. I adorned the shop with just a set of six tables and 24 chairs inside with wipe-clean surfaces. I adorned the walls with posters of pasta and scenes of Italian cities. I made sure the windows were large and decoration-free so people could see what was going on inside.

The banks, of course, being the generous organizations that they are, helped in every way possible. They made me put up my house as collateral while charging me exorbitant interest rates. These were the days before better business banking. Apart from that, they offered little assistance.

I sourced local farms for fresh produce, eggs, mushrooms, tomatoes, herbs, and above all, fresh garlic. I found a durum wheat supplier near a source of fresh, virgin olive oil. For everything else, we just used local wholesale suppliers, getting discounts and deals that suited both them and us.

Fresh pasta is made with durum wheat flour and is meant to be consumed within 24 hours or at least refrigerated until consumption. Dried pasta is always made with semolina flour, which gives it a tangier taste. Dried pasta can be kept for a very long time as there is no decay in its chemistry, and it will keep its freshness without loss of taste. I wanted to make nothing but the freshest pasta!

I did use something that was very new at the time. Computers were in their infancy. When I started my business, there was no email, Twitter, Facebook, internet, intranet, or world-wide superhighway. The only games available were Pong or Pac-Man, played on a large arcade unit. Absolutely everything related to running my business was on paper. I paid with handwritten checks.

As we made everything fresh on the premises, for the launch, I kept things simple. A menu of six long and short pasta shapes:

- Spaghetti
- Farfalle
- Conchiglie
- Tagliatelle
- Fusilli
- Penne

- 2 kinds of filled pasta - Tortellini with 3 Cheeses and Tortellini with ham and cheese.

We sold three sauces: bolognese, pesto, and a cheese sauce infused with herbs and lemon.

As an ex-musician, I wrote and narrated a couple of jingles and recorded them in a little four-track studio in Plymouth, arranging regular radio play to drum up interest. I had flyers printed and distributed them around the city. To advertise the shop, I visited pubs, bars, markets, and any place where people congregated. On opening day, we were inundated by two customers in the entire eight-hour day. It was far from the roaring success we had hoped for.

Back to the drawing board, big time. The solution was to send people out onto the streets and hand out tasting samples. That did the trick! Within a short time, the shop was turning over in favor of fair trade.

Another thing I learned early on was that it was warm to leave the door open. The smell of freshly prepared pasta and brewing coffee wafted out onto the street, drawing in the curious and those who were already converts.

Never satisfied, I looked for another opportunity. Being on the coast, Plymouth had an enormous naval college which overlooked the city from the hills above. A few miles away was the main cadet college in the UK, Dartmouth. They ate fresh pasta, and surely, we could provide it.

We shut the shop to the usual clientele and had an open house, inviting purchasers from both colleges, many local hotels, and anyone who might buy what we had to sell. We provided Italian wine, pasta, and coffee. The open house initiative was a great success and, of course, created another problem. How could we supply in bulk?

With the help of a local enterprise grant, we set up a factory on a nearby industrial estate. I built a 40ft by 20ft production unit with doors, windows, and a roof. Four more machines were purchased from London, and local staff were trained as pasta makers. From here, the range of pasta shapes and sauces we offered began to grow. We also perfected our packaging and distribution processes.

This, of course, led to another one of my many ideas. What about selling pasta at farmers' markets, which are the staple for fresh produce in that part of the country? Within a year, we had so many sales that I had a steadily growing intake of staff.

When I opened a second shop in the capital city of Cornwall, Truro, I applied for a liquor license and sold Italian wine and cheeses. I eventually turned the premises into a small delicatessen selling all types of Italian fare. This was the business model that was used when we expanded further.

This necessitated a few trips to Italy, where I set up deals for wine and olive oil, having them shipped over by the container load every few months or as required. What we did not use ourselves, we sold locally, keeping everyone happy and making a profit.

By the end of the 1990s, we had shops in Truro, Plymouth, Penzance, and Exeter. We were also servicing about 50 restaurants across Cornwall and Devon with fresh pasta and acting as distributors for a couple of Italian vineyards, cheesemakers, and olive oil producers.

Obviously, the hard work had been done, and the roots of the tree had been sunk into what I hoped was fertile and encouraging ground. At the time, I had looked forward to the future with great expectation and a huge dollop of optimism.

It was a few years later when that particular adventure suddenly stopped like a car crash on a rainy night. A particularly brutal and nasty divorce brought things to an untimely and abrupt end. Sadly, we had just signed a deal to supply some of the local and nationwide big-name supermarkets with pasta noodles, filled pasta, and a range of sauces.

A new, snappy logo was designed, along with distinctive packaging, to promote the brand. Luckily, because the business was by then a fair-sized operation, I was able to sell the name and the franchise for a reasonable price.

What has happened to the business since then? I do not know. It was subsumed into the parent organization and either run under a different name or dumped altogether. It is not that I didn't care; it is just that sometimes looking back can be rather painful when the only real way is the road forward.

The entire experience – good and bad – allowed me to grow as a person. To move as far away from the West of England as I could, and relocate to Eastern Scotland to continue to develop. I feel this is something you should do all of your life so as not to become stagnant.

I am now a writer. I enjoy the freedom and the opportunity to exercise my reclusive spirit that the craft allows.

This book is not an end-all, be-all definitive guide to opening a fast-food venture. I wanted to make it as readable as possible without going into the depths of financial boredom.

This book is simply meant to guide you along a path from concept to opening, and then to explore the possibilities of developing your initial idea into either an independently owned enterprise or a buy-in to someone else's established franchise.

I will leave you with one of my favourite go-to quotes:

"The beginning is always today." - Mary Wollstonecraft Shelley

"Popcorn is one of the only situations in which you eat the result of an explosion."

Demetri Martin, Comedian, Actor and Musician.

THE INDUSTRY OF FAST FOOD

To set the record straight, I may have stretched the truth in part of the introduction. In fact, the United

States of America did indeed invent the term "fast food" in the 1950s.

FAST FOOD THROUGHOUT HISTORY

But cast your mind further back than that. Say you were building the pyramids in Egypt. You normally did not have a lunch break. Unions were a long way from being invented, so you ate on the go in full view of your foreman, who knew well that you would drop from exhaustion if you did not put something into your mouth to keep you going. A provided lunch was not in your slave contract, so you brought beer, bread, raw vegetables, and a few dates to keep you going. This was the first "fast food."

The Roman staple was bread liberally coated in garum, a disgusting, foul-smelling fish sauce that was used on just about everything. Fast-food stalls called "popinas" sold bread soaked in red wine with stewed vegetables and meat. If you were poor, it was the only relief from the blandest of diets on which you existed. The rich, on the other hand, enjoyed dormice and vole; any small rodents, in fact, were fair game and a fine delicacy for the middle-class household. For the downtrodden citizen, it was back to the garum, essentially their quick, easy go-to food.

Between the 12th and 20th centuries, at your average beheading or hanging, you were cheered up between deaths with nibbles, things on sticks, pies, flans, pancakes, and pastries. Those who were about to be executed were so drunk on wine or gin that they didn't care. For the raging crowd, the delicacies that were provided for sale were essentially "fast food."

MODERN EVOLUTION OF FAST FOOD

So, now we get to America. Arguably, the first snack food, or perhaps that should read, "junk food," appeared at the Chicago World's Fair in 1893. The brothers Frederick and Louis Rueckheim had a great or crazy idea of marketing a product called Cracker Jack. They poured molasses over popcorn and peanuts, creating a sweet-and-salty combination that made them a lot of money when they began selling the product nationwide.

The first fully recognized fast-food restaurant, The White Castle, which sold nothing but hamburgers, opened in 1921 in Wichita, Kansas. It was unique because the food was prepared in front of you and not behind the scenes. Fast food, as the official term, was not yet invented. The White Castle restaurant was designed to be a high-turnover, high-volume, no-fuss establishment where you queued at a counter to place your order and were given eating utensils before you were seated. It did away with waitress service and cut frills to a minimum. The idea was to get you in and out as quickly as possible.

The first chain was, yes, you guessed it, the Mighty Golden Arches. McDonald's was introduced in 1953 in Phoenix, Arizona. McDonald's was first founded by the brothers Richard and Maurice McDonald in San Bernardino, California, in 1940. At first, it was a normal full-service restaurant until they changed the name and, in a flash of inspiration, called it a "Hamburger Stand."

This stand employed the same techniques as The White Castle to get 'em in and get 'em out as quickly as possible. It was not until they sold the growing business to entrepreneur Ray Kroc that it became the business it would become. A trademark for the big M was filed in 1962, and the infamous clown Ronald was born two years later. The invention was made with the express wish of attracting as many children into the establishment as possible. It was reasoned that the younger you get them, the longer you keep them.

It is estimated that the worldwide franchise of McDonald's 36K restaurants sells more than 100 million burgers a day, giving the American Way of Life global recognition. From Manchester to Moscow to Macau, consumers no longer look to their indigenous food; they simply take comfort in a bun and a mcflurry as the go-to indulgence.

Kentucky Fried Chicken, spearheaded by the finger-licking Colonel Harland Sanders, came next. Fried chicken, a staple of the Deep South, became the comfort food of the masses. The Colonel had sold chicken from his roadside establishment, Sanders Court and Café, in 1930, and prospered throughout the depression era. He latched onto and developed the concept that later became known as "franchising."

Whilst it was "all feathers and no chicken" for the disenfranchised poor of the nation, the Colonel prospered quickly. For him, at least, it was "chicken all the way to the bank."

The first KFC franchise opened in Utah in 1952 and has since spread all over the world. His down-home image was so popular that when he sold out in 1964, the new owners loved his Southern-gent persona so much that they made him the pin-up and poster boy of the relaunched company, making him one of the great American icons of the 20th Century. KFC has long been acknowledged as the industry's number two. It prospered because it was different. It was always chicken-led from the start, rather than the quintessential burger.

Not to be outdone, Burger King, Taco Bell, and Wendy's launched themselves in the early 1950s and 60s. Of course, that was only the beginning. The floodgates were opened.

Fast food not only took over America, but its hand opened, and its fingers spread out all over the world. It was almost as if the US Government had put a moratorium on war and violence, and had, instead, instructed the nation's food makers to conquer the earth by means of ingredients rather than blood.

America, if you like, is Americanizing the world for the ultimate benefit of Americans wherever they may be. It is certainly to the credit of businessmen that US-originated fast food is everywhere.

A Cultural Phenomenon

Eric Schlosser, a fast-food journalist and business expert, said, "Fast food chains spend a large amount of marketing to get the attention of children. People form their eating habits as children, so they try to nurture clients as youngsters."

Let's look at a bit of history here. This is simply a reflection on the importance of timing, historical or otherwise, and especially on personal timing and how it ultimately affects both life and you.

Fast food, as we know it, was really born in the Southern United States with the natural progression from White Castle to McDonald's to the good ol' Colonel and KFC. It was a food movement directly influenced by, and aimed at, young people who frequented restaurants and popularized certain food choices.

Running parallel to this development was the vast expanse of interconnecting highways that crisscrossed the country from the Atlantic to the Pacific, linking all points in between. More cars than ever were on those highways, with a huge upsurge of teenagers behind the wheel and driving those cars.

It was only natural that the phenomenon of fast food exploded because now everyone had somewhere to go, and needed fuel, not only for their vehicles but also for their bodies, to get there as safely as possible.

The idea of the rebellious, independent teenager did not exist. Prior to 1950, it had not yet been invented. You went from school to work, perhaps to college or university, but you did not differ from your parents' or grandparents' path. You worked, got married, had children, grew old, and died, just like all the generations that had gone before you.

Think about it. Is that not rather strange? Maybe the real teenager, as we know today, was invented in America at the same time as the fast-food industry? Teenagers never went through the rebellious teenage years, because society did not recognize them.

Fast food joints sprang up all over America. Some were single operator stops, sometimes open 24 hours a day, to make a buck from the passing trade. But it was the franchisers who knew how to do it better. They became this huge, rolling monster that, in a few years, was not content with its American homeland but set out to claim the world in its wake.

In Memphis in 1954, a 19-year-old truck driver was taking tentative steps into music, recording a throwaway single at Sam Phillips' Sun Studios as a birthday present for his mother. The recording genius knew talent when he heard it and got the boy together with some session men to cut his first proper track.

That boy was Elvis Presley, ...and the rest is history!

I hope you can see the analogy I am making that the three cultures emerged side by side.

Fast Food + Cars + Rock and Roll = Teenage Culture

The invention of rock and roll and fast, easy-to-get hamburgers were synonymous. They both fed off each other, becoming the lifeblood of the future.

It is a phenomenon called "Right Time, Right Place." It happens to all of us at least once in our lives. Ask anyone of a certain age what they can pinpoint in their life through major events. Ask any baby boomer where they were when JFK was shot, or when the moon landings happened, or, more recently, the death of Diana, Princess of Wales.

It is remembrance and familiarity that make the big fast-food retailers ultimately so successful. Wherever we are in the world, whatever we are doing, Colonel Sanders will always make us feel at home.

To succeed at your dreams, it is probably already aligned in a particular conjunction of the stars formed at your birth, hence your "Right Time, Right Place." Some of us are lucky, and a sad fact of life is that others are not.

There really is nothing you can do about it other than fight fate.

GLOBAL PERSPECTIVE

In Great Britain, before the early 1950s, our idea of fast food was the staple available on every high street in the land, which remains immensely popular today. That's typical British fish and chips!

Made of either cod or haddock, collated to within an inch of its demise, coated with a slimy substance of flour, salt, baking powder, and water, dipped in boiling fat to be served in a newspaper with soggy chips submerged in vinegar.

I am sure your mouth is watering in delighted anticipation even as I type this.

It was the staple food of, to put it plain and simple, the poor. It was a working-class treat after a night at the pub. It is, in most cases, indigenous to the UK specifically. There are franchise equivalents, all of which are individually owned.

As of December 2019, there are plans to launch a UK franchise by a company called Hero Brands. They aim to open 300 restaurants over the next 10 years, with what they call a "healthy alternative" to the genre and a new concept to a tired idea. Only time will tell if they are successful.

Chinese and Indian restaurants that metamorphosed, like so many butterflies, into staples of British fare, with much watered-down versions of the original and indigenous cuisines, came late to the franchise game.

The UK had the first successful franchise of the Lyons Corner House tea shops, with the famous waitresses decked out in a distinctive uniform, complete with a frilly apron and cap. They were the quick-turnaround establishments of their day, and although it was still waitress service, the whole ethos prospered on getting customers in and out as fast as possible.

Another successful franchise to make its way to the UK was Wimpy's. The original Wimpy's restaurants were born in Chicago in 1934. At its peak, it had about 1500 units worldwide, but something was always missing. The inferior burgers and buns were forever gasping for air in a sea of grease. They soon sank.

Wimpy's headquarters were moved to the United Kingdom in 1954 after being bought by the owners of the Lyons Tea House group. They opened the first "Wimpy's Bar" in London that same year. Sadly, they seemed to be stuck in a pre-60s time warp, one that never moved forward. Unfortunately, upper management seemed to lack the originality, flair, and forward-thinking needed to move the project forward.

The most popular UK success of the last few years has been the fast-food chain, Greggs. It was a bakery business that began trading in northern England in 1951. It began an aggressive round of acquisitions in the early 1970s and has over 1,600 outlets throughout Britain, 144 of which are franchises. They have opened over 90 in the last 11 months alone (as of December 2019).

Their success has been their high turnover, brand style, and strategic marketing to the "food on the go" crowd. The recent shift to low-salt, low-sugar, and low-calorie options has only boosted their profits. They hit the jackpot by creating a need to introduce vegetarian items on the menu.

THE EXPERIENCE OF FAST FOOD

Walk down any street, anywhere in the world, and you are inundated with advertisements of all shapes and sizes enticing you to try something new and desirable- perfume, jeans, TV's - but above all, food. The faster, the better. We live crowded together in huge disposable urban cages in a society that just throws things away. If you don't like it, you can just buy another one. The ultimate success of the franchise industry is that it allows you to do just that.

Let's make no bones about it. Fast food is not a *restaurant* experience; it is a *fuel* experience. The polar opposite of fast food is fine dining.

With a sit-down, full-service restaurant, the decor is imaginative and welcoming. The service by trained wait staff caters to your every need. The staff is headed by the front-of-house, who must be an expert in every aspect of the business. They employ a sommelier, a wine expert of the highest order, or at least someone who can tell a chardonnay from a sauvignon blanc. In the kitchen is a phalanx of chefs who have undergone years of training in order to bring you a meal that is as close to culinary perfection as they can achieve. It is meant to be an experience to savor.

On the other hand, fast food is meant to be an impersonal experience. Certainly, one that keeps human interaction to a bare minimum. The very mantra of the industry is that fast food is just that – fast. The psychology of the fast-food restaurant is simply: get them in, order, seat, and out again as fast as you can. Play the music loud, make the seats uncomfortable, and keep the décor simple and bare. You don't want people loitering about. You want their money as often as you can.

If you do not learn that lesson as quickly as possible, then this is the wrong career choice for you. Fast food is a service industry based on convenience and brevity. It rises and falls with how many people you can seat, successfully feed, and then get out the door again to replicate the experience.

Fast food works because it creates familiarity. Wherever you go, in any city in the world, you know what you are getting. Apart from some obvious regional differences, the dishes (a term used loosely) all taste the same. It is also comfort food. Never mind if you are a thousand miles from home; go into your favorite fast-food establishment, and you are transported back to the city and community you are happiest in.

The Globalization of Food

All modern food is an adulteration of the original. Indian food in Milwaukee is nothing like Indian food in Bangalore. If you eat Mexican food in a resort in Cancun, then taste it on the side streets of Mexico City, there is a huge difference. Sicilian pizza has no bearing on the slices sold in a New York deli. Regional food has all been watered down to suit the average palate of someone not from that country. It takes a seasoned traveler to know the difference.

As a planet, we are becoming increasingly aware that what we put into our mouths affects our health, mental health, and long-term well-being. We are being told daily that what we eat is, in fact, what we are, and that is true. Obesity is increasingly prevalent, most of it linked to overeating. Serious long-term diseases are being linked to meat consumption.

I am not an Astrologer, but I think that in the next 10 years, there will be a great change away from the custom of eating meat. Lobbyists are examining the global influence and emissions of bovine farming on the climate. It is said that if we eliminated the vast herds of cattle we eat daily, we could eradicate the damage methane causes to the ozone layer within 10 to 20 years.

Even McDonald's restaurants are supplementing their famous giveaway plastic toys with small bags of vegetables and fruit. Most of the bigger chain franchises are slowly becoming more vegetable-friendly than they once were.

Change is coming, and in that change will be a shift away from animal-based diets toward more vegetarian and vegan options. The younger generations are eschewing cigarettes and alcohol, and, certainly in Europe, a meat-free diet is becoming a very popular option.

With rising sea levels and climate uncertainty, plant-based fast food may be the way forward, as it has been for the past 100 years, but it may evolve into a hybrid or branch we are as yet unclear about.

"All our dreams can come true if we have the courage to pursue them."

Walt Disney

ENTREPRENEURIAL FLAIR

So, you have an idea? Sure, we all have those all the time. The knack is turning that idea into a reality. It is not that hard. Hard work, determination, and above all, luck is what you need.

Most people nowadays would not know a good businessman if he bit them in the street. They look ordinary. Unless they are wearing a great big badge saying "VIP," they go pretty much unnoticed - lost in the crowd.

POSITIVES

Entrepreneurs are self-reliant people. They want to dig their own furrow, not walk in someone else's. They know what they want, and pretty much how they are going to achieve it. Generally, they love a good challenge and are, by and large, optimistic people

Many years ago, I was in the film industry. I have been on many sound stages and countless sets. I am never ceasing to be amazed by the designers' and builders' combined talents. One was particularly memorable. There was once a huge life-size forest stretching as far as the eye could see. Caged in it was a pack of Alsatians (think German Shepherds) that would later be transformed into wolves by the graphics department. The Director wanted them to bond as a pack. The result in the final film was truly spectacular.

I mention this because that is what your regular, everyday entrepreneur does. He visualizes something that does not exist, but which is fully formed in his own brain.

They tend to be believers who dream of thousands of unconquered Everests. They are certainly learners who will never stop learning, striving to be better than they were yesterday, doing the same thing tomorrow in a different way.

Creative thinking and strong personal belief are other qualities they should cultivate in abundance. An entrepreneur should be a confident risk-taker who, if they have doubts about their own abilities, keep it to themselves. They should certainly be considered an innovator who does not take no for an answer.

NEGATIVES

Where there is a plus, there is always a minus to balance things out.

Entrepreneurs can also lose sight of their objectives and their duty of care to their customers because there is always something else on their minds. Too many projects really do spoil the broth. Never lose sight of that original goal. Do not commit to anything you are not sure of. Always communicate clearly and concisely and stay aware of daily market changes. Be aware that just because you might have decided on something, it may not be right, and that your time needs to be managed along with everyone else's.

You must weigh yourself up to see if YOU have what it takes.

How do you eat an elephant? One bite at a time!

That is the nature of your business. You cannot do everything all at once. It initially seems like a daunting task, yet it must be a very gradual process. Most good businessmen can turn their hands to most things or at least know someone who can do what they cannot.

Everything is possible. Starting today, get in the habit of eliminating certain words from your vocabulary. Start with the words "probably, maybe, and soon." Replace these words with "now."

Find your own words and get rid of them by surrounding yourself with an aura of positivity – even in the bad days.

Stop and think about the fear factor for a minute. Fear can be our greatest enemy or our best friend. You can be fearful about starting a business, but once you have taken that great leap into the unknown, it is the fear of failure that keeps you going. I am not saying that to deter you, but to motivate you.

In the early days, you are too caught up in the planning, doing, and running the business to do anything else. Then, the fear factor kicks in. Kick it out the door.

Even the most successful people you can name are frightened. It's fear that drives them. You have to learn to turn the fear into a positive, not a negative.

Being Original

Have you ever really thought about it? The good old hamburger has been lying to you all your life. It is not a "ham" burger at all. It's a "cow" burger. For those of you who might be unaware, "ham" comes from pigs, not cows.

But who would buy a "cow burger" with all its sinister connotations? "Ham" is far more user-friendly.

Some people would tell you that the horsemen of the Mongolian Steppes invented it so that they could eat whilst riding, their thoughts on plundering and pillaging ahead.

Others will say it is a derivative of steak tartare, just the raw ingredient bound together and cooked, then taken to Hamburg and adopted by the meat-loving Germans. Ships of the Hamburg line took millions of the dispossessed to America, where one enterprising German immigrant set up a series of "Frikadelle" stands on the streets of New York.

Of course, the hamburger is synonymous with America. Whoever's interpretation of history you may believe, the name and the familiar beef patties on a bun were born between 1855 and 1895. But it was at the St. Louis World's Fair in 1904 that it took center stage.

By 1916, a chef named Walter Anderson had invented the recognizable bun and, 5 years later, went on to co-found our old friend The White Castle. From there, it was simply history and progress.

But this section is not about the history of the almighty hamburger. It is about alternatives.

Just as no one needs another hero, I am pretty sure no one needs another hamburger joint. Take a walk down your local Main Street. Everything you could possibly want is available for you to eat. There's a new food for every day of the week and a food for every mood you might be in – sweet, sour, and everything in between.

The simple task for you is to find and serve a niche no one else has thought of. Somewhere, there's a gaping hole in the market that needs to be different, inventive, and most importantly, your own original idea.

There are still plenty of untapped ideas around. It is just that you have to find them. Maybe it's a new slant on an old idea. Maybe it's pasta, or a crossover between sushi and ice cream.

Above all, study others. Why is McDonald's so successful? Learn how they successfully did what they did with hard work, massive effort, and huge amounts of good fortune; you can do it as well.

BECOME AN EXPERT

Obviously, you are a foodie, a chef, or otherwise a very keen amateur who wants to make food your own. So, before you decide on something you may live to regret, read as many books as you can. Attend as many seminars as possible as you can. Become a master of the fast food that they are trying to sell.

Let's look at pasta again. There are thousands of books on the subject. Make yourself an expert on pasta. Make as many forms of pasta as you can. Small, hand-operated pasta-making machines cost at most $30. Learn the basics, and then experiment. Mix the dough. Change up the flavors and shapes. Make filled and non-filled. Become adept and enjoy the learning curve it offers. It is all education, after all.

Try this trick. Go to your favorite local restaurant and offer to do menial tasks for free. Offer to do some dishwashing, vegetable peeling, sweeping, and mopping, anything that will give you a feel for what you want to do. Gather some practical, real-world experience in the restaurant world. Remember, this job does not have to be in a fast food establishment, but it is preferable if it is.

Even consider taking a job at McDonald's, or its local equivalent, for a month to see what you can learn. You will see the business firsthand. You'll likely witness how some run smoothly whilst others operate in abject confusion. The complete picture will unfold before you, and all you have invested is a little time.

Talk to people. Family, friends, and if you are brave enough, go out into the street armed with a clipboard, talk to the food-buying public and ask a simple question. Is there a need for my idea in this town?

People love to talk, thinking that what they say might end up on the radio or social media, because, after all, you want their open and honest opinion. It might not give you the answer you were looking for, but at least it will give you some sort of idea of the market need. It is that need that will give you your startup idea.

You have to come up with something unique, an idea that is going to not only get you noticed by anyone who may wish to finance you, but more importantly, something that is new and unique in the catering industry in which you wish to work. I can only wish you well because that is a very, very hard task. If not, everyone would be rushing to do it.

BE HONEST WITH YOURSELF

An independently owned and run enterprise is when an individual or a small group of people come together for the common good, moving forward as a group. Together, surmounting and deal with the problems that arise as a team. They attempt to tap a market niche no one else has seen, then develop a product and food service that are totally unique to the person or people who proposed them.

For the readers who have gotten this far with me, for the rest of the book, no matter the type of fast-food establishment you wish to open, I will reference pasta, as it simplifies things a bit for you and me. The basic formulas are the same, no matter the choice of food that you serve.

Before you do anything, stop and think. Take days, weeks, months, or even years to think. Running a business is not something to be undertaken lightly. Years of hard work lie ahead of you, and many sacrifices will have to be made. Not everyone is up for either the task or the responsibility that comes with it.

Let's face it. Some people are unprepared for the leap of faith it takes in their own abilities to run a business. A monthly salary and a clearly defined set of objectives to work on far outweigh the overwhelming responsibility of going it alone and starting a business. It is a challenge that, after birth, adolescence, marriage, and death, is probably one of the biggest ones you will ever face. It is a journey not to be taken lightly, and whatever the outcome or rewards, it will change your life forever.

If you decide that you cannot see any way forward apart from the business route, then there are a few things you should look at before you make that final leap.

DEFINE YOUR STRENGTHS

First off, grab a piece of paper. Tear it in half. On one page, write "strengths" and, on the other, write "weaknesses." Here you will list qualities that are yours, not someone else's. Be honest with yourself and be blunt.

Yes, I know it's a hard thing to do, but this is essential for the life you are about to embark on. Forget about safety and the 9-to-5 routine that will become a thing of the past, and what you are now will go with it.

The above exercise is essential. If you are honest with yourself, it will give you a pretty accurate picture of who you are, what you need to change, and what you need to address to move forward. A firm road map is all you need.

Are you up to the challenge? Perhaps not, as it becomes a different ball game when it is you who is calling the shots rather than someone else. Also, do not underestimate the stress factor; believe me, it is enormous. Are there people around you whom you can talk to? Are there people you can try your ideas on? Are those closest to you really aware of the many years of struggle that are in front of you? This is all reality, as harsh as they may be to deal with. You have to face the facts in the cold light of day.

PLAN TO DEAL WITH SETBACKS

Plan for all eventualities. It is a stark fact that most businesses go bust within the first 2 years of operation, and food businesses are the worst offenders. Take it from me. There are worse things in life than bankruptcy. It happened to me 15 years ago, and I am still up and fighting.

What matters is how you decide to deal with the problems that beset you, not the actual problem itself. If you give in to it, then you are finished. If you accept that it has happened, and the sooner you deal with the consequences, the sooner you can get on with your next adventure.

Failure is not an option that anyone would choose; it is simply a sad fact of business life. Never be deterred.

You're the inventor of your own dreams. Make something else happen!

"I think that still is true of any business, which is basically research and development, that you probably spend more time in planning, training, and designing for things to go wrong, and how you cope with them, than you do for things to go right."

Alan Shepard, Astronaut, talking about the Aerospace Industry.

PRACTICALITIES OF STARTING A BUSINESS

No matter the direction you wish to take with your fast-food establishment, even before you start putting the business together, you have to weigh the options. These are the practicalities of running your business on a day-to-day basis.

REGISTER YOUR COMPANY

Your first decision is what sort of business entity you want to start. Your main choices are to be a sole proprietor or an LLC (limited liability company). This is a highly important step, as it legally protects you against all that may befall you.

As a sole proprietor, you are taking the weight of your entire business and its expenditure upon your own shoulders. That might be fine in the good times, but fatal in the bad.

With an LLC, the assets of the company are separate from your personal assets. The LLC stands alone in terms of taxes and your liability.

Before you do anything else, you must contact a knowledgeable lawyer and a reputable accountant. Also, contact a reliable realtor who knows the opportunities in your immediate area. These are specialists. They will help you identify any premises that are empty, for sale, or, sadly, being repossessed by a finance company or bank. These people are an invaluable source of material, experience, and advice, and they will, hopefully, guide you in making the right choices.

This is only one of the very many choices that you must make.

Find Your Corner

Above all, find an underserved niche in the marketplace. There is always one. I will come back to this point again and again throughout the book.

Finding a niche in the food industry is the Holy Grail. Produce something that is so new and different that it cannot help but be a success. Perhaps it is a vegetarian or vegan slant, perhaps it's grasshoppers and other edible insects on sticks, or maybe it's the ultimate gourmet fast food experience on the go.

Find your own corner and fight long and hard for it with the spirit and tenacity to overcome all of the problems that you will inevitably encounter.

START WITH SOCIAL MEDIA

I bring up the subject of social media because it is one of the major platforms for promotion that there is. It is imperative that you set up accounts on Facebook, Twitter, and LinkedIn, and, most certainly, set up a company website as soon as possible. This is all free promotion, which you should use and update as often as you can.

It is almost impossible to run a 21st-century business without using at least some of them, and the possibilities are endless. Even before you are physically trading, tell people what you are doing and the process you are going through to get the business up and running.

Sell the idea, build up a following, tell people your dream, and then keep telling them each step you are taking. Make them funny, make them informative, make them stand out from all the millions of words that are posted every day.

Apart from followers and likes, you will get interest in your project right from the start. So, use it as it is meant to be used for your own benefit and ultimate profit.

Location and Competition

Pick your prospective premises with care. Consider the area as a whole and the passing customers.

Are you near any major amenities, such as perhaps a bowling alley, ice skating rink, movie theater, or anywhere else that attracts passing customers?

Buying, leasing, or renting monthly are all options you will need to consider. The most important factor is, of course, to evaluate your competition.

Within a mile or so of where I live, there are 21 hair salons and about 6 florists. How the heck any of them turn a profit is totally beyond me. There is just too much competition for anyone to make a profit!

But of course, you will be selling a totally new, unique, and exciting fast food experience. Competition! What Competition?

How do I find my ideal premises? The answer is quite simply "location, location, location." You can find that location by driving around your potential neighborhood, spotting premises that are closing or closed, or fast-food outlets that are up for sale.

These can also be advertised in your local newspaper or, more importantly, in publications that weekly or monthly advertise such opportunities. Believe me. A good location is a great way to hook any bank manager who may be wavering on offering your funding.

Depending on the state of your finances or how much you have been able to borrow, you have three options:

- Buy
- Lease
- Rent

Buying is obviously very simple. You contact your lawyer, realtor, and your accountant, agree on a price with the seller, exchange contracts, and like magic, you could own a shop.

Leasing normally implies a fixed-term agreement between two parties. Again, a legal document that needs your team's approval. As a rule of thumb, it is better to buy than to lease if you intend to remain in that location for more than 7 years. Oh, to have such an accurate crystal ball!

Renting is a much shorter option. There is no long-term commitment; you rent from month to month, or in some cases, week to week. The downside is that the renter must give the rentee little or no notice to vacate the premises if there is a disagreement or a falling out. If you like living in a constant state of uncertainty, it is probably the option for you.

To achieve high-volume sales, you are going to need to survive; your business must be situated in an area with lots of opportunities for trade and growth, which certainly means a busy area, such as a mall or shopping complex.

If you choose a shopping mall, you will certainly have foot traffic past your window that is interested in purchasing from you. The downfall is that the need for fast food increases the later the hour is. Malls close early, just when your potential customers are out and about, so in many ways, it could be a disadvantage.

Branding

Michelle Obama, the wife of ex-US President Barak, said, "The problem is when that fun stuff becomes the habit. And I think that's what's happened in our culture. Fast food has become the everyday meal."

My father-in-law is a renowned portrait painter, and I hate him for it. I hate him because I envy his talent so much. It's a joke, of course. I admire him and his talent immensely. He is a dedicated man and in different times would have been lauded as a great artist. He does with a pencil and paper what we mortals can only dream of achieving. Sure, he has talent, sure he studied hard and works equally hard on his given talent, yet he is unique.

Everyone has a daily need, be it water, food, love. We all crave basically the same things that we are all committed to, and that sustains us and our bodies in good health and well-being. When we turn those needs into commodities, we enter the world of branding.

Branding is that instantly recognizable symbol. It's one that, whether you are in Cairo or Cincinnati, catches your eye and brings you everything you are familiar with. You can even imagine these famous brands in your head: The Marlborough man, Texaco, Coca-Cola, Lego, and Amazon. The list of brands that elicit instant recognition is endless.

In the film world, by the end of WWI, Charlie Chaplin had defined a character, the 'Little Tramp,' who bred familiarity all over the World. The baggy pants, the silly walk, the twirling cane, and the twitching mustache became the signature. He was recognized everywhere he went, and everyone knew the Tramp. This was the original instance of branding.

Look at McDonald's. You do not need to read the name, but just see the great big golden arches to know what the brand is. The same with KFC. The Colonel may have been in the army, although he never gained any rank. It was in 1935 that he was made an Honorary Colonel by the then Governor of Kentucky and sported the goatee and Southern gentleman clothing in order to look the part. You only have to glimpse his silhouette to know what the chain is.

I am sure someone somewhere is currently designing a band that will be a world-beater.

It is of the utmost importance that you settle your brand image right from the start so that it becomes instantly recognizable in a customer's mind's eye. Instant logo recognition is an essential tool for brand growth.

Your mascot must always be synonymous with the brand, giving it a clear direction for the future. Should you appear in TV ads, no matter how localized, customers will see them, so they will see you.

The big franchises have always been big on image:

- Wendy's – The owner's eight-year-old daughter. Remember the "Where's the Beef?" campaign of decades ago?

- KFC – Who else but the Colonel himself?

- TGI Friday's – Well, Thank Goodness it's Friday!

- Taco Bell - Hey, think outside the bun.

- Pizza Hut – Makin' it Great. You can instantly recognize a Pizza Hut from its signature hat-shaped, red-roofed restaurants.

- McDonald's has a whole parade of revolving characters that they pull out for various photo opportunities.

    - I'm Lovin' it. All-round Slogan.

    - Ronald McDonald – That infamous rascal and all-around funster.

    - the

    - Grimace – A purple blob of nothing and Ronald's comedy-foil.

    - Birdie the Early Bird.

    - Fry Kids.

    - Mayor McCheese.

    - Officer Big Mac.

- Professor (McDonald's)

I am sure you can think of a thousand more, but better still, go and create your own one before someone else does!

WHAT'S IN A NAME?

The first thing to consider for your fledgling business is a name. This seems an easy decision. Yet it is of tantamount importance. Whether you have global ambitions or not, it will follow you around until it ceases to exist, or you do whatever comes sooner.

Firstly, check Companies House – or your country's equivalent of it – to see if the name you want is already registered. In the US, each state registers companies, so check with your state government. If the name appears to be an already established company, you obviously cannot use it. It is owned and registered to that company and its directors for their sole use. It means that the copyright has been assigned to them and cannot be tampered with.

Another quick way to find if a company name is already in use is to do a quick web search for that business name. If you can find a website for it and the name and business are too similar to what you want to start, you may have to alter your branding direction.

All books, films, CDs, music, the internet, and everything on it are copyright of an individual, organization, or corporation. So is everything else in the world. So, just remember, if in doubt, do not touch it by a mile. It will only end in litigation.

Copyright is a hugely important fact for you, as is your business name. Copyright that name by adding a small symbol © clearly showing that name, that logo, and the year. Once you or someone you have paid to design an original logo for you, it will remain your intellectual property in perpetuity.

Of course, always consult a professional on copyright law, such as your attorney.

When John Lennon of the Beatles died, his wife, Yoko Ono, trademarked his name and secured copyright protection under her jurisdiction. Only she can agree if someone can use the name. 100 times out of 100, she disagrees and litigates vigorously. There are numerous recorded instances of Ms. Y suing the most inconsequential business in the smallest hick town on the planet for using the name Lennon!

IMAGE IS EVERYTHING

Logos are an integral part of establishing a brand. It is what makes them stand out. Brands have instant recognition. They have power; they can and do practically anything they want to conquer the world and wield considerable muscle both financially and politically. Their influence on politics reaches all the way to the vast amount of corporate tax they are not paying.

I am not suggesting for one moment that you can immediately compete with the majors because you can't, but you can think like them. Right from the start, think long and hard about the image and the impression you wish to create; it is extremely important.

An old cliché says to think outside the box. If you personally have no artistic ability, you can either pay someone to develop your conceptual idea or, the way I do everything, do it yourself!

After all, you have control, you have the vision, and it's your baby. No one will be more committed to it than you are.

Put that logo and those colors everywhere. Place that image on your packaging, storefront, windows, interior, and uniform.

We live in an age when you can do it all, from designing your own logo and letterheads to mocking up menus and flyers for general distribution. Everything is possible in this computerised age. You do not need to be a design genius; you just need an idea, and your PC will do the rest.

Invest in purchasing Adobe Acrobat. This software is a great tool for expressing yourself. If that's a little too pricey, there are lots of free programs available. Surf the web, download, and play around with your ideas!

CONSISTENT ORIGINALITY

But remember that your concept, the marketing kind, of course, not the food one, has to be absolutely unique. I cannot stress the importance of concept and design enough.

Bringing consistency to your ideas and brand is what ultimately makes you stand out from the crowd. Your core values as a business are defined by it, and certainly, if you wish to grow even to the point of opening another outlet in another town, it should become the cornerstone of all you are trying to achieve.

Just as you should take care of the recipes that you are preparing to sell, you should always follow the same pattern. People will come back to you time and time again because of how your food tastes. Should you be fortunate enough to repeat your fast-food experience elsewhere, keep it exactly the same as the first.

THE BUSINESS PLAN

The art of presenting a good business proposal is tricky. The watchword is *be prepared*. Be as prepared as you can before you approach anyone about your business idea. Above all, be at the top of your game before you approach the Bank Manager/Financier.

Undoubtedly, this is the most important function you undertake at the very beginning of your journey. It provides, for those interested, a complete set of aims and objectives for a specified period that you will complete. It goes without saying that it is a snapshot of your business intentions for those you hope will invest in your idea.

Impress your idea immediately on page 1. Impart your qualifications for running the business and your boundless enthusiasm for it. Go on, sell yourself.

First, you need to talk about money. What your budget is, what you need it for, your projected earnings, your premises, everything that you have information about. Include your startup costs and your projected running costs for up to 5 years. Any information, in fact, that will help them make an informed decision about your business acumen.

Give a detailed description of not only your chosen name but also what food type you intend to specialize in. It will also outline your experience in what you intend to do. Obviously, if you are a trained chef, include your certificates and references to previous employers.

Include as much information as you can on the research you conducted and the results it gave you. Put the information in graphs or tables to impress readers and make it easier to digest.

Everyone loves pictures, so insert as many as you can — certainly, the more information that you include, the better. You need to explain the business's structure. It can be you and your wife, you and a partner, or even just you. Everyone who will view the plan needs as much information as possible to be as accurate as possible.

When you put your projections on paper, they become a perfectly simple mathematical equation. When dealing with profit and projected earnings, the equation is this:

Profit = Income - Costs

If you do not feel confident enough to do any of the financial parts yourself, talk to your accountant or lawyer; that's what you are paying them for. Also, talk to anyone and everyone so you get good advice. Always ask as many questions as you can. It can be exhausting, I know, but it's a learning curve. No matter the stage you are at, you should always be thinking and looking forward.

I cannot stress enough the importance of making your business plan as interesting and readable as possible. Put yourself in the Bank Manager or Financier's place! They see at the very least, 100 proposals a month asking for money. It's their job, after all. So, it is your job to give them something that literally blows their socks off. Make the proposal stand out. They want to see flair, inventiveness, and above all, uniqueness. If you put that onto paper and convince them of its soundness by your own charisma, then you might have a chance.

You will rarely get a decision on the same day; they generally like you to sweat a bit first.

I would recommend a website called Law Depot (https://www.lawdepot.com/). They will actually put together a complete business plan for you. They can provide you with a free template to use as a basis for your presentation.

I say "basis" because you should not use the plan as is. It is the dumb and dumber way to succeed. Present it to any financial institution, and they will instantly know that you have put little or no thought into the planned proposal.

To recap on the parts of a good business plan:

- Executive Summary
- Key Personnel
- Market Research – The NEED
- Marketing Plan
- Financial Information
- Running Costs
- Growth Expectation

"An entrepreneur tends to bite off a little more than he can chew, hoping he'll quickly learn how to chew it."

Roy Ash. Co-founder of Litton Industries and political advisor under Nixon and Ford

DEALING WITH THE BANK

Eric Schlosser, journalist and author, said, "A generation ago, three-quarters of the money used to buy food in the United States was spent to prepare meals at home. Today, about half of the money used to buy food is spent at restaurants -mainly at fast food restaurants."

So, you have created a killer business plan that you are totally committed to and happy with, and you have booked your appointment with your friendly neighborhood bank manager.

He is simply waiting for your call and will most certainly invite you to lunch at the best restaurant in town. Of course, over the exquisite meal, you will not talk business; that can wait until you are back at the bank. No, he wants to know about you, your hobbies and interests, your family and friends.

After two, three, or four bottles of wine and a few brandies, you stroll leisurely back to his office. Before you even open your briefcase, he has agreed to all your requests. He obviously thinks your business plan is the best thing he's ever seen and will most certainly make you very rich, which will reflect glory on him because he gave you your start.

Then, of course, you wake up.

It has all been a dream, and sadly, the reality is really going to test you and your dream.

Banks are there for one thing: to make money. Oh, but not for you, though, but for them. They need to feed the demands of shareholders, investors, and the favored in the community.

You, as a small businessman, if you are indeed successful, are just the icing on a cupcake rather than a more substantial cake. They will always prefer the former over the latter.

There is no point in being smart; just be honest and professional. Present your case in the best way you can and figuratively exit stage left with as much dignity as you can. Bank managers have seen charlatans all their working lives. They can smell them before they even walk through the door, because it is their job to do so.

BE AUTHENTIC

A friendly warning. In all your dealings, be as fair and as honest as you can be; there is no point in trying to be underhanded, sly, or devious. If you are proud of your product and your own personal standing, do not lie about it; it will eventually taint what you are trying to do.

I have never understood "business tricks." You will invariably be found out. Getting found out means your character is demeaned, and your good intentions are thrown to the wind. It is far better to have a good name and be known for sound business practices.

In the end, a hard deal is better than a devious deal. Treat everyone you meet with honesty and fairness. You would hope they would do that in return.

Some businesspeople like to play the game. I have never had any interest in the game throughout all my years; with all the various things I have done. You either want to do a deal with me, or you don't. Stop messing around. You will most certainly have to take that approach with your suppliers at some point, and certainly with your own staff.

Never play games; it never gets you anywhere. Certainly, never waste people's time. If you do, you will never get a second chance.

BE RESILIENT

Elbert Hubbard, US philosopher, writer, and artist, once said, "To avoid criticism, do nothing, say nothing, and be nothing."

In war, if you never put your head above the parapet, it is certain that you will never be a target for the enemy. The same is the same in business. If you never try, well then, you never fail. Either take a risk or most certainly stay where you are.

Starting any business on your own means taking that risk. You may succeed, but you may equally fail. Do all the research you may. Read all the books you can. But nothing beats the heart-wrenching difficulty of failing. Sorry, it is an essential part of life.

It is not in the failure that you should wallow. It is not what happens to you. It is how you choose to deal with it. Believe me, even with the most positive outlook in the world, it takes a very, very long time to get back on your feet again. I have a personal and very painful experience with this.

So, the bank must be approached with a practical mindset. You are somewhat naive if you think that this person, whom you have probably never met before, is simply going to give you what you request within minutes of meeting you for the first time. I think not.

Banks hate startups. Why? Because 35% of them fail in the first year and a further 35% within five years. Make no mistake about it. You are entering a very competitive and tough business that takes no prisoners and leaves few survivors.

That is what banks do. It's their job to lend money. Banks do not lend money to people who think they can recoup the startup money from the first few years' profits. Why? Because there will be none. Even the most professional of business plans is only an outline, a set of financial aspirations and dreams. They are not the reality that is yet to unfold.

When a dream fails, the bank wants to be assured it will get its money back. There is an old saying that is pretty universal: "A bank will give you an umbrella on a sunny day and take it back when it rains." Sadly, it is a simple lesson in business life.

Alternatives to Bank Loans

Understand that the bank wants security above all so it can recoup any losses without incurring losses itself. It is what they do. It is why they are successful. It is why they have it, and you don't.

They will take all the liquid assets you offer them - cash, stocks, shares, your car, your yacht, your Rolex, your set of Rembrandt etchings, and above all else, the equity in your home. These things are all assets that can be sold should the business default. The bank's protection is all that matters, not you and your dreams as an individual.

Establishing a line of credit is a little easier if you have the above and do not exceed the agreed-upon amount. There are alternatives, such as borrowing from friends and family. That can be risky unless they themselves are stable financially. Plus, they know where to send the hitmen if there is a problem! Never go to a high-interest loan company or pile debts onto your credit card in desperation. It does not work and will only end in despair and endless years of misery. The alternative is to seek out an independent financing group or company. They tend to be rather more imaginative than the straightforward banking community. They tend to look more at the overall proposal than at a straightforward balance sheet and profit-and-loss forecasts. Your local business incubator and certainly your accountant can give you a list of names.

The moral of this story is, of course, the old Boy Scout's motto of "Be Prepared." Be prepared for every eventuality - plan for it, expect it, and deal with it when it happens. It is far easier than you think if you have done your homework and know what to expect. I will talk more about banks later in the book. If you are getting nowhere in finding financing, try your local Chamber of Commerce. They will have a raft of alternative finance schemes that they can discuss with you, and it is their job to point you in the right direction to find that source. Good Luck.

"A recipe has no soul. You, as the cook, must bring soul to the recipe."

Thomas Keller – chef, restaurateur, and writer

OTHER COSTS TO CONSIDER

INSURANCE

So what is the point of insurance? Well, unless you are going to be cooking in the open air with no combustible items nearby, using a stream to wash dishes, serving everything cold with plastic kitchen utensils, hoping nothing goes wrong, then maybe you don't need insurance. There is every need for insurance. You never know what could happen when you're dealing with staff, equipment, and customers.

These types of insurance coverages may be called different things in your country of residence. You may also need coverage beyond the examples I have shown below. It is general advice. Talk to an insurance adjuster to gain more information about your specific restaurant.

The types of insurance you may want to explore include:

- Public Liability
- Employer's Liability
- Product Liability
- Equipment Liability
- Professional Indemnity

Public liability insurance is basic business insurance that you will need, especially if you are serving fast food to the public, where they are expected to eat on the premises. It will cover legal expenses and compensation if you have to settle a claim brought against you, should any member of the general public suffer personal injury or property damage while on the premises as a result of your direct or indirect actions.

Employer's liability insurance is a must, even if you have only one member of your staff team. In the UK, you must have EL insurance of at least £5 million, or you are subject to a daily fine that can run into the thousands. There are certain circumstances in which you do not have to be covered by it, but talk to your lawyer, who will point out the positives and negatives.

Product liability insurance is another essential must-have. It does not matter about your thoroughness in the cooking process or in cleaning the shop; accidents happen every day! It also covers you against claims like food poisoning, Salmonella, or allergic reactions. Even if you personally did not make the meal, the business and you are liable.

Equipment liability insurance covers your equipment. Ovens burn out — fridges short-circuit. Fryers burst into flames. This covers you not only for replacements but also for any of the above occurrences that result in the loss of valuable stock. It will be replaced.

Professional indemnity insurance, while not compulsory, is advisable. It covers negligence by you or a member of your team. Such negligence may include breach of copyright or the use of, intentionally or unintentionally, someone else's intellectual property, i.e., their own special recipe.

I have explained the basics; follow it up with your own research, but remember this one fact: *you can never have too much insurance.*

LICENSING

You must have at least a working knowledge of the law as it relates to you and how you run your business. Obviously, you have an attorney who is there for the big things, but you must be aware of the small things.

Contact your local business affairs office. They can provide you with a breakdown of topics such as general civic legislation, water, gas, and electricity operators, and their good conduct practices.

Before you start, you should also have investigated:

- Food Standards
- Business Licence
- Food Service Licence or Health Department requirements
- Certificate of Occupancy from the Fire Marshal

In simple terms, a business license allows you to operate and run your business in a certain area. It involves registering your business name and paying an application fee. This might be to the state, county, or city where your business is located.

In the UK, no restaurant can begin trading without a Food Service License. It is granted once you have been visited by a Health Department official who confirms that all food-handling requirements have been met. In certain circumstances, they will insist that the owner should have completed a food safety course or training program to have a food handler's permit.

A Certificate of Occupancy shows that the premises where the business is situated are safe for staff and customers to enter. It will also indicate the maximum number of people that can safely occupy the building at one time. Exits must be properly marked, and fire suppression systems must be in place.

These certificates will differ from country, state, and county. You will have to check your local ordinances to ensure you comply with the law.

Equipment

Masaharu Morimoto, TV Celebrity chef and culinary expert, said, "Japanese chefs believe our soul goes into our knives once we start using them. You wouldn't put your soul in a dishwasher!"

So, we have the money in the bank, and you have the storefront. All the lights stretching in front of you, as far as you can see, are set to green. You have the building. Now you have to fill it and begin the real task at hand.

Once you have decided on your idea, it is up to you what you put into your empty store. Obviously, you should include ample storage space for dry and wet goods, as well as considerable wall storage, in the kitchen area. Think about bathrooms for your customers and the same for your staff.

Whatever you do, do not scrimp on the practical cost of the things that you cannot do yourself. Some things are beyond the remit of even the most intelligent and practical person, no matter what they may think they are not.

Do not do it yourself, and under no circumstances get your sister-in-law's half-brother to fix the electrical or plumbing. In fact, anything, just because he is cheap. You will only live to regret standing in the burnt-out remnants of your still-smoking dream or the flooded basement that has ruined all your valuable stock.

You are going to have to draw up a list, first of the essentials, then of the peripherals. Of course, the essentials will have to include cooking equipment such as ovens and fryers. Before you even start thinking about that, think of the overall layout of the kitchen.

Go to a specialist retailer in catering equipment. Going to your local DIY store to save money is not really an option. Most mass-produced kitchen equipment meant for home use is not built to withstand the rough treatment meted out in your average working kitchen. Apart from that, stainless steel is easier to clean and does not harbor bacteria in hidden and unexpected places.

You really should settle for stainless steel, wipe-clean surfaces with lots of counter space. Remember that space is one thing you are going to need a lot of. You will need space to move freely, space to cook, space to prepare.

I would caution that you check your local building codes and zoning laws. Some authorities require a minimum distance between the counter and ovens to ensure an accident-free environment. This regulation depends on your locality and current laws.

Each kitchen will be set up differently from the last, taking into account the needs of the type of fast-food establishment you plan to run. A pizza place will have a different set of requirements from a burger place, as will a place selling fresh sushi or pasta. Do your homework.

Here is a list of items to consider in your new kitchen:

- Hard Goods – Ovens, stoves, grills, fryers, and microwaves.

- Cold Storage - Ice machines, large or walk-in freezers, a selection of refrigerators.

- Work Surfaces – Countertops, preparation tables, cutting boards, food tables.

- Miscellaneous Kitchenware – Frying pans, pots of various sizes.

- General utensils – Tongs, ladles, scoops, a selection of cookware items.

- Furnishings – Tables, chairs, booths, counter stand, display stand, display refrigerator.

- General items of décor that will give consistency to your branding and theme.

- Soft drink vending machines

- Dispensers – for cutlery, straws – make sure they are paper, remember sustainability.

- Miscellaneous items – Anything you may have forgotten. And believe me, there will always be something you forget.

A point-of-sale (POS) machine is now essential, regardless of the size of your establishment. Gone are the days of a written order and a cumbersome cash till. A fully computerized system allows your orders to be processed quickly, logs ingredient inventory, and alerts you to what to reorder.

It also allows searchers to find your location through any number of search engines. Whilst it allows you to take a myriad of payment options, from cash to all credit cards, chip cards, and digital wallets. There are plentiful options out there. Find the one that works for your organization.

Don't scrimp. If you can't buy the best because it's too expensive, you can go with lower quality and upgrade once the business is steady. You could consider renting equipment. This is becoming a viable option for many startups. There are certainly many companies on the market willing to meet your needs.

Search the web, read catering magazines, and go to any number of wholesalers in your area. Most catering wholesalers also have an online presence, which gives you the widest choice of equipment. Again, talk to people. Visit other fast-food establishments and see what they offer.

Take note: there are always many catering sales held by auction houses, both large and small. Check out places and dates, and go along. It is well worth the time. The sales consist of company bankruptcies, retirees, repossessions, and people who are purely upgrading.

Be selective. You do not have to buy everything from one place. One or two pieces may be competitively priced as well. It is also good to remember that, on the whole, catering equipment, like a new car, loses a significant portion of its value before it is even installed. Since the depreciation rate is the same for new and old, you might want to consider buying the latter rather than the former to improve cash flow.

All these elements should be factored into your business plan.

"You were born to win, but to be a winner, you must plan to win, prepare to win, and expect to win."

Zig Ziglar – motivational speaker

RUNNING THE BUSINESS

It goes without saying that you must check out your personal liabilities before you do anything else. You have a responsibility to those you serve and work for to get it right from the get-go.

You must implement a code of good practice that treats food with the respect it deserves and what your customers deserve. Respect the proper cooking temperatures for ingredients such as beef, chicken, sausage, eggs, fish, and vegetables. Know how these ingredients should be stored, as well.

Everyone should be aware of cross-contamination, how to correctly store cooked and uncooked food, and how to correctly prepare them when they are near each other. Food such as fruit and vegetables should have their own designated preparation area, as should raw and cooked meats.

You should also consider both your health and your employees'. You should always stock an up-to-date first-aid kit, fire extinguishers, fire blankets, and other fire-suppression systems. These are required by law to be kept up. Either take on the task or designate someone as Safety Warden. Appoint someone who can handle minor accidents and has good knowledge of medical practices, such as CPR, to keep on top of the daily safety needs of your establishment.

Send home any staff who are ill. This is especially important if they have diarrhea, vomiting, or a fever. Also, be aware that the flu bug can be passed on through contact with the many surfaces it may have touched. Wounds should be treated immediately, cleaned, and covered, well away from any uncovered food or preparation areas.

Regarding cross-contamination, make sure food is always covered and that all ingredients, regardless of their nature, are kept in reusable tubs with airtight lids. Use the tubs for the same ingredients, as even when cleaned thoroughly, they will retain a film residue from what has been contained in them.

CLEANLINESS MATTERS

It does not mean that just because you cannot see something, it is not there, nor that it is not going to ultimately kill you. Bacteria are one of those unseen killers.

Your normal neighbourhood: unfriendly bacteria are single-cell organisms that live in, on, and under every square centimetre not only of the earth but also of everything that lives and moves on its surface. So you, your establishment, and everything in it are literally riddled with these unseen, silent killers.

Singularly, they can be dealt with. As a coagulated, joined mass, they can cause listeria, hepatitis A, E. coli, and Salmonella. All of which could potentially kill you or your unfortunate customer.

There are millions of unseen germs on the normal human hand. Healthy regimens must be in place from day one in your workplace. Hands must be washed frequently, especially after using the toilet, shaking hands, and any skin-to-skin contact.

You must instill in yourself and your staff that a regular handwashing regimen is as essential to their well-being as it is to your customers' well-being and health.

It is impossible to impress on any food vendor the vital importance of hygiene to the ultimate success of your business. It is up to you as the owner to be an example.

Failure to implement strict rules about food safety, hygiene, and clean operating practices will very rapidly land you in court or out of business - or both.

One of the great pains about any form of commercial catering is the endless round of cleaning. It never ends – floor sweeping, table wiping, dishwashing, and just the sheer effort to keep on top of it all. You may have been lucky to invest in partially self-cleaning equipment, but believe me, self- or non-self-cleaning equipment still needs cleaning at the end of the day.

If you have available funds, invest in a good washing machine to wash your cleaning towels. Make it a habit to clean things at night before you go home and, in the morning, before you start. It is really important to impress on your staff the need to keep on top of cleaning. One shift will not thank the last one if they have to clear up any leftover mess. It is up to you to train your staff well and keep on top of it all.

Unless you have employed someone specifically to keep on top of the chore of cleaning, set up a system so that all staff members take turns cleaning regularly. I would also urge you, as the proprietor, to directly lend a hand as well It is called leading from the front, or the art of leadership. Empty the trash, clean tables as soon as they are vacated, and keep up with things regularly.

Health inspectors are everywhere. You will not recognize them as they do not wear hats with "Health Inspector" on them, or jackets with the logo of your civic or town council. They are far more subtle, blending in with customers, buying a meal just to check you out, then returning shortly afterward with a laptop or tablet under their arm in order to confront you with all the things you are doing wrong.

Of course, if there is anything wrong, as there will be in even the most spotless of establishments, you will be given an allotted number of days until the health inspector returns. He will check to see that his demands have been met. Do not ignore him as he has the power and authority to levy a heavy fine on the business, or if he is in a really bad mood, to close you down altogether or at least until the problems are rectified to his satisfaction.

I remember in the first place I opened. I had to replace and heighten a kitchen door. I am pretty short, 5'7', and set the lintel and aperture 3" shorter than they legally should have been. The lesson learned was that not everyone comes from a long line of short people, as I do!

Even at the planning stage, your dry runs before opening day, and certainly on opening day itself, should ensure a workable cleaning routine is in place. No one likes a mess, and certainly not your customers. Whether the majority of your food is eaten on the premises or is taken away to be consumed, keep it clean.

"Cooking requires confident guesswork and improvisation—experimentation and substitution, dealing with failure and uncertainty in a creative way."

Paul Theroux – travel writer and novelist

EXPANDING THE BUSINESS

Ok, grab that crystal ball, and let's look into it. For you, we see that you are some ways down the line, and things are looking good.

So, you have made a roaring success of your brilliant fast-food idea. You have cut your loan and balanced the books. Your profits are far greater than your losses. Better still, you have learned the intricacies of your trade. You have a well-trained staff who are reliable, loyal, and committed to the business's success.

Even better, the bank manager is happy and has taken you out to discuss other opportunities. All in all, you are on the up and up!

If you have succeeded in one location, with one concept, a great team, and a great idea, there is obviously no reason why you should not succeed in another.

- You have devised a successful template.
- You have a recognizable name.
- You have a recognizable logo.
- You have a recognizable brand
- You know that people are drawn to your product.

If you are happy and content, and you are happy and content to run a successful fast-food place that meets your need for personal fulfilment, then I am truly happy for you. Let's leave it at that, and I can only wish you well with the rest of your long and successful career and ultimately your life.

Sadly, for most of us, a one-trick pony is never enough. The old saying goes, "always have a horse in reserve should you need to ride another one." If you have an idea, just one of them, you can always have another.

Boredom is the sure-fire killer of all ambition.

Pick another town, another idea, or maybe the same one. Choose a different idea; should you feel the urge to tackle a different concept. Pick the same one if you have long-term ideas of building a chain on the same principle.

I don't say everything will be easier, because it won't. You will have the same problems, only this time you will be ready for them with a wealth of experience under your belt. The bank manager will certainly be more willing to fund you as he will be confident in your abilities, as he will have seen the results, as, of course, you will have seen them, too.

No matter how many shops you have, they all have the same problems, but they are only magnified by the establishments you have. You have achieved it once. You can do it again!

BE CONFIDENT

My late mother had a great saying that I was taught at an early age, and one I would like to pass on to you: "There is no such word as can't." Meaning, of course, that you can achieve anything you set your mind to do. This isn't necessarily true, but it's not far off the mark, either.

With a little luck, we can set our minds to do just about anything. That is, if Lady Luck is behind us, and if we possess that special something that raises us up from the ordinary.

I spent much of my youth in the film and music industries. In doing so, I was privy to many secrets, gossip, and confidences. I had a friend, a well-known makeup artist, who had worked on a number of major feature films, including the James Bond franchise.

She never ceased to be amazed at how the magic was created by a collective crew, for the good of all, and the same goal of a finished product. Her thought was always that what she was doing was simply fooling people, which is what movie magic is made of.

Ultimately, it is a matter of confidence and how you present yourself to people.

The secret to the success of your venture is to make it look effortless and easy, although it may be the toughest challenge you have, or ever will, face. It's all about the magic of the illusionist, the art of smoke and mirrors.

You must have the innate confidence in yourself and in your unique abilities to create the dream.

Never undersell or underestimate yourself. You can and will surmount any obstacle or any challenge put in front of you if you have belief in yourself.

The leap of faith from point A to Z is a very small one indeed, as long as you have the drive and the tenacity to carry it out. Go do it!

THE ROAD MAP

Think about the concept you have developed, and recreate your steps from where you are now back to how it all began.

Ask yourself these questions:

- How did I do it?
- What did I do right?
- What did I do wrong?
- What is the next step?

Think about your current location. How can you improve it, expand the business, and move on without the huge cost of another startup in another town?

GO MOBILE

You could go mobile. Think about a food truck or catering opportunities.

With a mobile outlet, the appropriate licenses, and so on, you could take your successful product out of your own area and into brand-new territory. It will prove to you that you are not just a one-hit wonder and give you an idea of how you could slowly grow the business. It has a number of benefits. You are getting your product and your name more exposure with free advertising to boot, and it is also developing a product need.

SELL WHOLESALE

Look at a wholesale use for your product. Supermarkets are always on the lookout for something new. You only need to visit any of them regularly to see how often they update their lines. They also have dedicated product development teams whose sole function is to actively seek new food ideas. Could it be yours?

Again, you can take that next step. Use some spare room in your shop. Rent or lease a small warehouse, more machinery, and hire more staff. In this manner, you have another way to expand the business without incurring the expense and hassle of other expansion methods. You already created the product; you just have to send it out in a new way.

This route is also a great way to gain name exposure in your immediate area, which creates further brand awareness.

SELL FRANCHISE RIGHTS

You could take your fast-food idea and create an opportunity for others to buy into it, too. Maybe they would want to run and own a "Bob's Chicken and Waffles" in their hometown?

Setting up this structure is legally perplexing and would, for sure, require the services of a good attorney who knows about corporate law and contracts. The decision to launch your own franchise is not a decision to take lightly.

FUTURE TRENDS

"What we need is an entrepreneurial society in which innovation and entrepreneurship are normal, steady, and continuous." - Peter Drucker, US business consultant

No matter the food option you are offering, things will always change. Let us look at some expected changes in the fast-food industry over the next 5 years.

HOME DELIVERY

There has been a huge change in the number of fast-food outlets offering delivery services. All the major hitters are now offering it. Pretty soon, it will be the norm rather than a novelty, thanks to the added convenience for fast-food customers.

A risk it may be, as it is certain to cut what is already a very slim profit margin to the bone. When considering how to implement a delivery service option in your business, the costs to you and how you will pass those costs onto the consumer are the number one consideration.

When adding delivery, you could:

- Partner with a food delivery service such as Waiter or Uber Eats.

- Purchase your own branded fleet of vehicles and drivers, so that you control the rates, routes, and quality of the food as it's being sent out.

- Hire independent delivery drivers, much like pizza places do, usually charging a flat delivery fee plus tips.

These choices will vary greatly depending on how much capital you can invest in your delivery service and the kind of experience you wish to offer (pun intended!).

OFFER HEALTHIER OPTIONS

People are more aware of their health than ever before because what we eat is what we are. The list of foods that will give you a heart attack, diabetes, high blood pressure, or a stroke is longer than Route 66.

The point is, we are lectured by our health practitioners about the risks of being unhealthy, and we probably realize that we drink too much and smoke too much. Certainly, with the enormous rise in global obesity over the past few years, we all eat too much. So, what do we collectively do?

We all look towards healthy options for the food we put in our mouths daily.

The vegetarian and vegan options are becoming an increasingly attractive alternative for the health-conscious many.

Do not be surprised when either a big industry player or a young upstart decides to throw their hat in the ring and start a new global venture along these lines.

Perhaps the answer will be an organic alternative, with an emphasis on fresh, healthy, sustainable produce, put together in a fast-food format.

It all boils down to health and how to maintain it, even when it's under the banner of fast food.

ORDER AHEAD/MOBILE ORDERING

There is also a growing trend in the fast-food industry: ordering ahead.

Several of the majors, including McDonald's, have rolled it out, making the whole fast-food experience even faster and more convenient. Apps have been designed to allow food to be ordered for pickup at a precise time and at the most convenient location.

Whatever the next innovations, they will come. It is only a matter of time and progress.

"The best way to predict the future is to create it."

Peter Drucker - Management consultant, educator, and author

POINTS TO REMEMBER

You are creating a fast-food outlet, not a fine-dining restaurant.

Get customers in and out again as quickly as possible.

Keep your overhead costs low and your standards high.

If something goes wrong, it is up to you to fix it.

A business is only as good as its best ideas.

You are its best idea!

I hope you have enjoyed reading the first part of this book as much as I have enjoyed writing it. Now that we have looked at the independent business model experience, I want to go through the mechanics of growing your fast-food brand into a chain or buying into someone else's franchise.

"Make your team feel respected, empowered, and genuinely excited about the company's mission."

Tim Westergren, Pandora Radio executive and listed as one of the top 100 influencers in the world

PART TWO: FRANCHISES

To franchise or not to franchise, that's the question. Whether you want to start and run a new fast-food business or expand your empire by franchising, we will examine what it takes.

FRANCHISES

We have already discussed the history of fast food, the nature of the industry, and how it is made to a standardized formula that is consistent no matter the location.

It has furthered the on-the-go culture we are embroiled in, ensuring that it is consumed in a hurry and on the move. Most of its produce comes from a centralized depot and is cooked, in some cases reheated, and served and delivered in accordance with company regulations and standards. Fast for the customer and fast for the staff, too.

With huge promotional and advertising budgets and aggressive marketing campaigns, the industry has drawn a lot of flak from health-conscious community members. Nevertheless, in the US alone, it is estimated that over $100 billion is spent on fast food per year.

It was Isaac Singer, the inventor of the humble Singer Sewing Machine, who gave the world the first franchise opportunity as he merchandised his handiwork across the United States and then the rest of the world. Unable to supply the heavy demand for his product during the mid to late 19th Century, he sold his idea in blueprint form to interested investors. They used his name and concept. He, in turn, used their money to expand and grow his initial concept even further.

Remember, this was the age of the great westward trek, when pioneers left the East in wagon trains pulled by oxen or pushing wheelbarrows from New York to Utah. Along with walking, cooking, and shooting Indians, they had to be self-sufficient, with cloth, pins, scissors, and a Singer brand sewing machine.

During the Great Depression, Howard Johnson introduced the concept of the franchise restaurant. He installed soda fountains, dotting them from San Francisco to Sacramento, each the same as the last, yet run on his principles by a different team in a different city.

It was not until the franchise concept was applied to the fast food industry that the US became the world leader.

CHOICES

I want you to think a little about the overall concept of the franchising system. No doubt you bought this book thinking it would give you all the answers to the many questions you want answered.

If I have succeeded, then I have failed in what I have tried to do. My hope and aim is that it poses more questions than it answers, because more than anything else, dear reader, I want you to think very deeply about the choices you are making.

As I stated in the beginning pages, I asked you to draw up a list of your personal strengths and weaknesses as a tick box to see if you have what it takes; to see if you could hack the cold light of day decisions and the sacrifices you were prepared to make on your road to entrepreneurial success.

I ask you to make another list, this time for or against taking on a franchise. Never mind the practicalities, we will deal with them in due course.

With the taking on of a franchise, you are leaving behind the free world of the independent businessman, where you have made your own decisions and decided your own fate, and lying down to take on the mantle of the "corporate beast."

The definition of a corporation is loosely "a company or group of people bound together in common good, authorized to act as a single entity in law." One of the great anomalies of US law is that the corporation is viewed as a single entity, a person, if you like. It has all the freedoms of a person and can be sued or litigated against as one.

The corporate ethos is probably something very different from your own. It comes with a different set of values and structures, a particular way of seeing and handling certain situations that you have either never looked at or would never condone in the first place.

Most fast-food companies have "Bibles," instruction manuals to be followed to the letter. You have no choice in the matter. It is simply what is expected of you and those you employ. If it says you wear a uniform, a name badge, and a hat, you comply with all three and wear them without question.

It all depends on what price you put on something and how much you are prepared to toe the line. Say you are running your own business, and you put a $3 price tag on a basic, no-frills cup of coffee. You take on a franchise and are told, no questions asked, to sell the same cup for $6. It's a matter of compromise.

Remember, above all, that you are buying the brand name. You put the work in it to be successful, and you will emerge a star!

WORTH THE COST

It really is down to individual preference. Everyone who plays cards would hope the deck that is in their hand is stacked in their favor. To a certain extent, you are getting that when you take on and invest in a franchise.

Business is all about mistakes, and paying for a franchise can help you avoid them. What you are getting is something that instantly works. It's like having a baby and not having to deal with the preschool years. Instantly, the child can walk, talk, be toilet-trained, and feed and dress themselves.

A franchise is very much like that; it provides you with a tried and tested proven method for success, built on someone else's mistakes and experiences.

You, as a new entrepreneur, will spend more time worrying about the garlic and tomato sauce rather than getting on with the nuts and bolts of setting up the business. If you have someone else's plan right from the start, then you follow it. You follow their operating system. You accept their formal training. You are interested in their approach to technology, overawed by their purchasing power and the style of their brand marketing, not to mention their network of like-minded fellow franchise owners.

Yes, you are paying a lot of bucks, but you are also getting a lot back. You are not going to be allowed to fail, even if it is all "tough love" from the company's side.

By hook or by crook, you will succeed by fair or foul means. They have too much invested in both the franchise and the brand ever to allow that to happen without bloodshed.

And it will certainly not be theirs, either!

"Don't worry about failure; you only have to be right just once."

Drew Houston - CEO of Dropbox

WHAT A FRANCHISE IS

Let's be frank about the franchise game. Firstly, take a sheet of paper and write down all the franchises you know. You will soon realize you need a bigger piece of paper than the one you have.

A franchise is defined as a business opportunity that devolves into a many-headed hydra. It is an enormous pie, cut into segments, primarily focused on market share and current and future growth, even though it is not the team that may have instigated the original concept.

A franchise opportunity is quite simply the granting of a license that allows the purchaser of that license to use the original company's knowledge, processes, and trademark. There are a whole lot of ways to look at the franchise game.

A typical definition would state that a franchise is a business in which the owner licenses the right to operate a particular company, along with its products, services, branding, and overall knowledge, for a fee. A franchisor is a business that grants licenses to operate under its terms and conditions to numerous franchisees, whose services vary from offer to offer and from business to business.

So, you have reached the point where you are considering the franchise option. As with running your own fast-food venture, you have a lot to think about. It is not always the case that the option is the most successful, yields the highest profit margins, or is even best for you. The bottom line is, "How much is this going to cost?"

It is third-party transaction money in exchange for knowledge, familiarity, and a proven brand that will, over time, make you a considerable amount of money, if you follow the proven rules, of course. It gives you the use of the name, the trademark, and, of course, the symbols associated with the business.

In most cases, in exchange for obtaining the franchise, the franchisee pays the franchisor an initial startup fee plus a periodic percentage of profits. You do it their way, under their model, their guidance, and most certainly, their direction.

It may seem easy, which, of course, it is not, but franchises are certainly a very popular method for those who wish to start a business and operate within the competitive fast-food industry.

BIG NAMES

Jefferey Gitomer, author, trainer, and business speaker, is quoted as saying, "Customer satisfaction is worthless. Customer loyalty is priceless."

Is big enough good enough? Or is bigger, or even the biggest, the best of all? Because of their very nature, they do not cancel each other out.

So, what is the world's biggest food franchise, then? It must be McDonald's! Sorry, but it's not. It's now Subway. Yes, I know how a simple sandwich can compete with fillings of your choosing, humble the mighty "Big Mac."

In June of 2019, it became the world's largest franchise, with a total of 44,852 outlets worldwide. Subway has had a meteoric rise since Fred DeLuca borrowed $ 1,000 from a friend and opened "Pete's Super Submarines" in Bridgeport, Connecticut. He led the franchise's growth until his death in 2015.

He hit upon an idea, ran with it, and succeeded, as did all of the big-name food giants. Subway will be toppled, in time, to be superseded by another bearer of the crown.

Everything is fluid in this industry. Big today, or bigger tomorrow, it matters little, because everyone has their allotted time.

Search the web for new trends and be aware of them. Keep your eye on the Trade papers for any long-term trends. Read *Entrepreneur Magazine,* which lists the top 500 fast food earners, but there are far more opportunities than that.

INDUSTRY INNOVATION

Jim Rohn said, "If you are not willing to risk the unusual, you will have to settle for the ordinary."

It is said that necessity is the mother of invention, so innovation must be its twin sister, as they both go hand in hand. Invention is creating the new and unique, and the act of innovation is the bettering of the original.

Never mind all the inventions that were made over the past two or three thousand years. First try, they got it wrong. It broke. It fell apart. It disintegrated into small, inconsequential pieces. The person who had to watch this failure just didn't leave it there. No, they went back to the drawing board and tried again until they got what they were after. Not perhaps achieving perfection, but at least a stab at it.

Michelangelo, the Italian artist who, amongst other things, gave us the statue of David and the paintings on the Sistine Chapel. It was the Pope who originally asked him to give the ceiling a couple of coats of emulsion paint, just to freshen it up, but he had set to work and painted a great deal of his original design before he realized that he was on the wrong track.

He used the words himself, "If the wine is tainted…throw it out!" He hated the original, and it was not until he defaced and destroyed it, went back to new designs, and completed the masterpiece that is viewed by millions every year. It was a true innovation. He was not happy with the original invention, so he bettered it.

So, it is the same with the art of fast food. The original is never good enough and can always be improved upon. Look at the best creators in the world. They always strive to improve. So must you.

"If you can dream it, you can do it. Your limits are all within yourself."

Brian Tracy

MONEY MATTERS

This is where we have to talk about stark realities. If you're considering buying into a franchise, you must certainly have deep pockets. You are going to need considerable access to a financial tap if you are to consider the most popular franchises.

Because, as I have already mentioned before, you are buying into an already well-established concept that is someone else's baby. The first thing to remember it has to be your money. You cannot go to a bank or a financial advisor and borrow it. It is simply not allowed.

Startup costs, cash flow considerations, and your overall potential to earn enough to have a reasonable living come down to doing your homework. Do not try to set your sights too high. It is a learning curve. Sure, you will make mistakes; everyone does. Knowing how to learn from it is the trick you need to master.

As I have already said, and will undoubtedly say again, no website, book, or advisor can give all the information you need. Get a head start on your competition and learn more about your business than anyone else. It is the only way to succeed.

Have a meeting with your account and lawyer and take their advice. Franchise agreements can be very complex.

Even the most basic of agreements has three major clauses, all dealing with payments.

CONTRACTUAL MATTERS

The buyer must purchase the controlled rights of the franchise, which include the trademark and the company's trading conditions, restrictions, and codes of practice. Which, of course, they must abide by.

The buyer will pay the franchise owner for any training and advisory services they receive. It is normal for the buyer to undergo a certain period of training to learn the values, principles, and aims of the parent company. Equipment and impartial advice are also factored into the overall equation.

The buyer will guarantee the franchise owner a percentage of the franchise owner's business sales. Make sure your attorney reviews the contract for gross or net profit-sharing. Make sure that your % is based on the business's net rather than the gross. It will make a huge difference to your overall profit margin.

Depending on the type of deal you sign, it is generally understood by both parties that you will never own the working name. The franchise owners will never own your Business. Have your attorney clarify this before you sign anything.

No matter the contract you sign, it is always a temporary agreement with an expiration date between 5 and 30 years. There can be serious consequences if either party breaches any part of what they have signed, whether through intentional violation or premature termination.

Wherever you are in the world, check your local legislation as all franchises are regulated at the highest level of government. These bodies set out a legal disclosure provided to every prospective buyer, laying out all the relevant information about the company they may need. It is basic protection that fully informs the purchaser of all the risks, benefits, and limitations of the investment they are considering.

As an open and informative document, it will also list the fees you are liable to accrue, including the suppliers and approved businesses you are expected to use.

FRANCHISE STARTING COSTS

You want personal freedom. You want the proven, tried-and-true formula that leads to success. Above all, when buying into a franchise, you want someone else's blueprint that takes away the need to make the same mistakes everybody else did.

If you embark on a fast-food business without support, training, or guidance, the odds are really stacked against you. At least with a franchise, you are a slight margin in front of the competition.

You must simply weigh the advantages against the disadvantages. You have the advantage of a ready-made business operation, complete with products, services, and in some cases, employee uniforms. All the planning and thinking have already been done for you, which takes away that hassle. The franchisor may even offer support throughout your and your staff's training, as well as a list of company-advised suppliers. It may be a formula for success, or a contract with the Devil, for it gives you little territorial control.

We have examined that the fast-food industry is loaded with pitfalls and failures. This is not necessarily through any great fault of the owner. It is purely down to extraneous circumstances, one of them being luck and another one being fate. There are circumstances that we do not foresee. Consider what would happen if the major employer in your town were to close down and lay off most of the workforce. You have just lost the great majority of your clientele.

Illness, sudden death, divorce - all these things need to be confronted. All small businesses, no matter what they sell, have an absurdly horrendous rate. Only about 30% of any type of business in any sector you would like to think does not make the 10-year benchmark. Even if it does succeed, it is because you have become a jack-of-all-trades, a conjurer, a clown, a lion tamer, and a ringmaster all rolled and wrapped in your own skin.

Turning your dream into reality will take years of hard work and self-sacrifice, with very little to show for it apart from a hole in your heart and, if you have any money left, an even bigger hole in your bank account.

So, then, perhaps the franchise world is for you if you have the money.

Below are listed the overall startup costs of 7 of the world's most popular franchise options as of December 2019.

- McDonald's
- Subway
- Wendy's
- Domino Pizza
- Taco Bell
- KFC

McDonald's

With a McDonald's restaurant, you are buying the best, so you should expect to pay the most. You have to be rich already to even think about it.

To simply get your foot in the door and be even remotely considered to be a welcome part of the great worldwide McDonald's franchise operation, you need the bare minimum of $995,000 in non-borrowed personal resources (and in the UK, just short of £860 thousand).

The normal way is buying an already existing restaurant direct from them or from the current owner/operator. You could find one that is well-established, and the change of hands is seamless, as long as you have the available cash. You can build from the ground up, but that is where the enormous figure comes from. You have to put down 40% of the overall cost, as opposed to 20% for one already operating.

Ask yourself a question. When was the last time you saw an empty McDonald's?

While the company may not offer any financing options, they do offer a comprehensive training program with ongoing training and an international support system to cover all eventualities. This is not an option. It is a must. They have an established brand and a substantial reputation to protect and they protect it to the hilt. There is a one-off franchise fee of $45,000 and a service fee of 4% of gross sales.

Subway

The subway was founded by Dr. Peter Buck, a nuclear physicist, and his friend, Fred de Luca, in Bridgeport, Connecticut. Yes, it's the USA again. By serving a well-made, high-quality, fresh product and keeping operating costs low, they soon prospered.

Currently, they have 43,000 stores worldwide across 110 locations, offering a franchise package very much along the McDonald's lines. It differs in that it offers interactive online training courses called "The University of Subway."

One thing to note about Subway is that, having come this far, they are always forward-thinking, which is a great sign for survival. In 2017, they implemented the Fresh Forward initiative. Like McDonald's, they have a rigorous vetting program and insist that all franchise owners attend an intensive course when they begin and an ongoing program of further instruction.

It is strange that, as they are currently the largest worldwide franchise developer, having overtaken the Big Mac in 2017, they have the lowest startup costs among major brands. The $15,000 in startup costs, which include construction and equipment leasing expenses, range from $116,000 to $263,000 (Company figures as of July 2019).

Royalties and fees paid to Subway are based on gross sales minus sales tax. The royalties are 8% to Subway and a 4.5% advertising fee paid to the franchisee advertising fund (Company figures as of December 2019).

All in all, Subway seems like a pretty safe bet and a well-constructed forward projection if you have the startup funds available.

WENDY'S

Wendy's, which began operating in Columbus, Ohio, on November 15th, 1969, was already franchising the name out to prospective buyers just three years later. It was the first food operator to develop the drive-thru window; the introduction of the slogan "Fresh, never frozen beef" and the invention of the salad bar only increased their early success.

To join the crew, you're going to need very deep pockets indeed. They require that your minimum net worth be $5 million and that you have $2 million in liquid assets for a multi-unit or franchise group. There is also a franchise fee of $40,000 per restaurant, a royalty rate of 4%, and an advertising rate of 4% of gross, not net, sales.

- The application fee is $5,000
- Background check fee is $325 per person
- Technical assistance fee of $40,000 per restaurant
- Local advertising is 0.5% of gross sales

There are many factors that influence the additional development costs for a new restaurant, including, but not limited to, real estate costs, building size, design features, local labour, building supplies, and permitting.

The estimated total investment required to begin operation of a new restaurant normally ranges from $2,000,000 to $3,500,000 (December 2019).

They offer basically the same package as everyone else with regard to training and ongoing development for you and the business, with an attractive set of incentives and support for those who wish to take up the challenge.

DOMINO'S PIZZA

Domino's Pizza is a predominantly English brand. It differs from the rest in that it is both a fast-food delivery service and an on-premises franchise. As of January 2019, they had 1261 units in six European countries.

Their selling points are speed and freshness, with mobile deliveries handled by a fleet of scooter drivers. In some cases, they offer free delivery if they are not delivered by a specified time.

I spent some time sifting through a lot of company information, but none of it was particularly helpful in terms of how to actually acquire a Domino's franchise. Nothing was really applicable, apart from the stark message that the minimum investment was 120,000 Euros and the total investment required was 280,000 Euros. So, you can make what you will.

TACO BELL

Taco Bell is a Mexican fast-food concept that was founded in the early 1950s as Taco-Tia food stands. Going through a few false starts, the first real Taco Bell restaurant opened in Downey, California, in 1962. By 1964, the concept was franchised, and global domination was just around the corner.

Glen Bell, the company's founder, sold the organization to Pepsi in 1978, which then subsequently sold it on to YUM! Brand in 1997 – the world's largest restaurant system.

It has become the go-to name for those who want a fast-food version of a Mexican food experience. Whether it is considered authentic or not is really up to personal taste. Yet they have a truly global reach, with a surprisingly high number of profitable franchises in Spain.

It has been very successful in attracting the youth market, as it has established a prominent position in the sports field, especially in American football. The company has sponsored a number of teams throughout the USA.

Taco Bell is built on traditional drive-thru and counter service, as well as an online platform and mobile app.

They have been very successful with ongoing, innovative ad campaigns that have benefited all franchise holders.

To get in the door, you will need $750,000 to start, then a total investment of $1M-$3M, with a minimum net worth of $1,500,000. There are no financing options available, and they offer the usual training and ongoing help packages.

KENTUCKY FRIED CHICKEN

KFC is now part of the YUM! Group with more than 18,000 units in more than 115 countries, each one headed by a chef preparing the traditional secret herb and spice recipes that the Colonel devised more than 70 years ago.

With the Colonel logo, it is an instantly recognizable brand, offering a worldwide protective umbrella for its franchise owners. It is also estimated that more than 12 million meals are served each day, providing instant security and stability for any franchise holder.

To become "finger-licking good," you will need an initial investment of $750.00 and a net worth of $1,500,000. There is a franchise fee of $45,000 with a total upfront investment of $1,309,000. The royalty fee is 5% of gross revenue, and the advertising fee is also 5% of gross revenue.

This is only the tip of a very large iceberg. Every type of food choice is available as a franchise startup, and every option is open to you, as long as you or a consortium of investors has the available funds.

OTHER PROFITABLE VENTURES

I wanted to look at just 5 of the most profitable fast-food franchises in the US market. Although the average startup costs were, in some cases, comparable to those of the major players.

Of course, the benefit is that these companies are on their way up and will grow considerably over the coming years. Whereas with many of the more established franchises, they have reached a certain saturation point in their markets and localities, with simply more of the same fare on offer.

New ideas and new choices will lead to a new breed of entrepreneurs.

WINGSTOP

So, who would have thought that a 1930s aviation-themed restaurant would catch on? First opened in 1994 in Texas, the franchise chain specializes in anything chicken – wings, boneless strips/wings, with a wide variety of dips, sauces, salads, and fries.

Through a series of trial-and-error mistakes, they have compiled a varied menu plan, always stripping away what is not working and continually innovating.

They are continually looking for new slants on the chicken business and are one of the players to watch for the future. In 2018 alone, their profit increased by almost 5% after their wholesale prices dropped by 23%.

Their minimum investment is $1,200,000, of which at least $600,000 must be in liquid assets.

JERSEY MIKE'S SUBS

Jersey Mike's Subs has a basic concept: to supply its customers with the freshest ingredients in a sub sandwich, prepared for them as they wait. They are keen advocates of the work-life balance and are also very keen to see franchise owners give back to the community in which they work.

They have implemented the "Mike's Way" program, a commitment to the community and customers. This is probably the reason they have won so many industry awards for quality and service.

Their website contains a full breakdown of costs and conditions, but you are looking at startup costs of between $237,000 to $766,000.

Krispy Kreme Donuts

Would you like more sugar with your sugar? If that answer is a resounding YES, then opening a Krispy Kreme franchise is definitely for you.

82 years ago, Vernon Rudolph began mixing his donuts in North Carolina and never really looked back. A rapid

expansion plan galvanized the company, propelling it to nationwide growth and then to rapid overseas growth.

Of course, as with all franchise operations, there are the for-and-against columns to be balanced. You could be looking at an 80% gross profit margin, but that is offset by the start-up cost.

You need a mere $275,000 to $1.9 million for that pleasure. This is far higher than most of its competitors. These figures are the good news. In reality, you need a net worth of $5 million just to post your application. You then must allow the organization to check your bank statements. They insist that you are a seasoned franchise owner with considerable experience in owning and running one or more restaurant outlets to a successful high point.

You are responsible for buying fixtures and fittings yourself - everything from work stations to donut machines. They will help with these costs through internal financing. And as a subsidiary, you will be paying 4.5% of your profits until you cease trading.

When all is said and done, Krispy Kreme is a pretty safe bet. In the most recent reports, it was noted that store owners could average between $ 60,000 and $ 70,000 a week. Even with the enormous outlay, if you have the startup cost, very few entrepreneurs will sniff at a $3 million turnover a year.

Firehouse Subs

It was only to be expected that this fast-growing line of restaurants would be conceived by the sons of a Fire-Chief. The Sorenson boys opened their first Fire Station in 1994 in Florida.

They came up with the concept that each establishment they opened would be different from the previous one, ensuring that each would offer a unique experience in décor and in food.

They have grown considerably in the US and Canada, and even in Puerto Rico, and have recently set their sights on Europe and the Far East.

Regarding the start-up cost, it is quite moderate compared with many of their competitors. A modest investment of $ 50,000 to $80,000 will get you the franchise. They undertake an extensive credit check and a review of your credit score and form an Ltd or Incorporated Company before they make a decision.

They have a unique concept that seeks to run an organization on ethical grounds, whilst giving back, involving the community in what it does, and using profits for the community's betterment. From their 2000 units, they have awarded something like $45 million to community projects, and especially – and who would have thought it – fire-related ones, of course.

DAIRY QUEEN

Originating as a soft-serve ice cream joint in Illinois in 1940, it soon expanded into other ice-cream-based products before adding chicken and dips to the mix.

They have developed a multi-branding strategy, mixed fast-food styles and tastes while retaining the Dairy Queen logo. Limited locations offer hot dogs, barbecue beef, and pork, but not hamburgers. While full-service locations offer the usual fast-food fare, they also operate under the banners of Grill & Chill, Orange Julius, and

Dairy Queen Brazier, each offering a combination menu to suit almost all tastes and budgets.

Last, but not least, they have also developed the Texas Country Chain, specializing in the "Hunger Buster Burger," the "Dude Chicken," and "Belt Buster," along with assorted tacos. It is unsurprising to find that there are more Dairy Queen restaurants in Texas than in any other place in the world.

Should you wish to become a part of the Dairy Queen Family or any of its many subsidiaries, the initial fee is $45,000, with a recurring royalty fee of 4% and a fixed 20-year term. Your recurring marketing fee is between 5-6% of gross revenue. Your total investment will be between $1 to $2 million.

Again, your liquid capital must exceed $400,000 for a single unit, and your net worth must be $750,000 for a single unit, plus that amount again for any additional units you may take on.

The above are just examples referenced from the available online research carried out in December 2019. They are going to change from country to country and from circumstance to individual circumstances. All the above dollar amounts are guidelines, and you should expect to pay more if you decide to go through a broker rather than directly to the franchise offeror.

LESS EXPENSIVE FRANCHISES

Here are the startup costs of eight of the world's least expensive franchise options as of December 2019.

Always remember that every coin has a flip side. It's the same with franchising, where there is an expensive option, there is always a cheaper one. Below are some of the cheaper fast food franchises available as of December 2019.

Being mostly recent startups, they have youth on their side. There is a lot of room to grow the idea. One of the great things about being in on the ground floor is that if you are successful, the only way is up.

They may not be really what you are looking for, but they are an option, and a safe bet at a low startup cost. If you run one of these successfully for a few years, get experience, and that all-important cash flow under your control, any franchise company or bank manager is going to see that you have what it takes to bite off a bigger dream.

Champs Chicken

This is mostly a Southern US chain with pretensions to grow much bigger. The owners brought their own family recipe to enhance the flavor of fried chicken, shrimp, and catfish. With a motto that proclaims "Blues, Brews, and Bird," and a carefully chosen décor for each of their stores, they are expected and expecting to go much further.

They currently have just under 400 units on board since 1998. The startup will cost you a franchise fee of $9,000, with a total investment of up to $349,000. Your net worth and liquid capital should both be $ 35,000- $ 65,000.

Ongoing fees include a royalty fee of 6 to 7.5%, with an advertising fee of 1.5% of gross profits. At a glance, this seems like an affordable choice.

YUM YUM DONUTS

This franchise is a little over 20 years old, but it seems to be a good price. This donut house started in Los Angeles, California, in 1971.

California may be its biggest market, but its expansion dreams do not stop there. They are based in Industry City, California, in a centralized production facility where they make and distribute the chain's basic ingredients.

To open a single Yum Yum, you will need between $3,400 and $ 44,700, depending on location. The initial franchise fee is $0. There is currently no yearly renewal fee, with 5% ad and royalty fees. The initial training period is quite short, a mere 16 hours, and as they do not offer exclusive territory rights, you might find yourself competing against yourself.

Certainly, a springboard in preparation for better things. Or perhaps a lifelong passion. Your choice?

CHECKERS/RALLY'S

Checkers Drive-In Restaurants is one of the largest double-drive-thru organizations in the US. Operating in some 28 States, they specialize in hamburgers, hot dogs, French fries, and milkshakes.

Having been around since 1985 or 1988, depending on who you ask, they have expanded slowly. However you approach it, this franchise is not the cheapest. The fee for each location is $30,000. The initial investment in operating is between $435,000 and $630,000.

You must also have a minimum net worth of $6,750,000 lying around unused, and pay a 4% royalty on net sales. For that investment, you are likely to have an annual gross return of somewhere in the region of $800,000.

Training includes an intensive five-week in-store training period and ongoing support from a dedicated business team that assists with site selection, construction, and ongoing guidance, especially regarding cost-saving, pricing, and quality control. You are also covered by a comprehensive marketing strategy through

TV, radio, and social media, and you basically benefit from every form of marketing strategy that the company can put together for you.

BASKIN ROBBINS

While it was founded in 1945, it may be an oldy, but it's a goody, too. Formed in Glendale, California, it sells its 31 flavors in over 50 countries.

They give customers a sample of the flavors on offer until they are sure there is one they want to buy.

They may charge an initial franchise fee of $25,000 for a 20-year term, but they require an investment of $93,000 to $400,000 in overall startup costs. 5% of gross sales as a royalty fee and 55% of the gross fee as an ad fee.

They favor multi-unit investors over anyone else and have a rigorous vetting program before they open their arms for a welcome hug.

At least the above options give you the idea that there are alternatives to the big players, ones where you do not have to put yourself, your family, and your ambitions into penury. Again, conduct thorough research as there are plenty of other options out there. You may be pleasantly surprised at what you find.

"Customers don't expect you to be perfect. They do expect you to fix things when they go wrong."

Don Porter – Management consultant

THE CORPORATE CULTURE

Corporations anywhere in the world are built on the same foundations. It does not really matter if you are selling hamburgers, cars, or washing machines. Whether you are Suzuki, CBS, or Dupont, you are instilled with a hard work ethic. Hired after you graduate, you are slotted into the corporate jigsaw. Certainly, with regards to the Japanese workforce, you are then a company man until you die.

It was the Japanese who formed the original corporate culture. In the 1970s, they coined the term *karoshi*, meaning "death by overwork." So ingrained were they in the company they worked for that they devoted their lives to the organization, spending extra hours, no holidays, early mornings, and late nights. Some even took to living in the workplace, grabbing sleep, eating junk food, and virtually disowning their families so they could be seen as giving their all for the company.

Of course, you can only keep that lark up for so long. They died in their droves or were so ashamed at what they perceived to be their failure by not keeping up with the killer schedule that they committed suicide. Even today, Japan has one of the highest rates of suicide in the known world.

The salaryman joins a company, works an average of 80 hours, spends 6 days chained to their desks, and, of course, never leaves that position until death by a heart attack, terminal illness, or stress. Being fired is virtually unknown, so is sick leave, and, in most cases, holidays.

In reality, the salaryman may be at work for 18 hours a day, but he is not actually working. As various studies have proven, he achieves far less in that time than the average Joe who puts in an 8-hour day.

That is really not the point, as it is to be seen rather than to do that which matters. In corporate culture, it is about knowing that the boss notices you on the premises rather than about what you do for the company. That is the most important thing. Your contribution, thereby, becomes irrelevant to its success or failure.

This idea migrated to the USA, and it is now a factor in business life: you are expected to dedicate yourself to the company. If you want to enter any franchise operation, you have to view it almost as giving up your soul and joining some sort of strict religious cult. The successful franchise owner must live and breathe the company's ethos 24 hours a day, seven days a week. There are no half-measures, no prisoners taken, no surrender accepted. It is the company's way, or it's the highway.

There is little concern about the individual and any personal wants they may have. You are a company man, and you are expected to tow the company line in all your dealings. As a representative of the company, you are a figurehead, someone in the community to look up to and aspire to. You must and will spout the company Bible at every opportunity and defend the company in all its dealings.

One of the great pluses for the corporate cultures of both Japan and the US, with regards to the food and the service industry, is that they leave most of the rest of the world on the proverbial starting blocks. There is a pervasive desire to please, to assist, to help, as if politeness and consideration are all part of the customer-oriented experience.

Look, you cannot get that big, no matter what franchise you are, without a strong corporate ethos. The company is everything and all. If you do not swallow that whole and believe everything you are told or read about, then the company and its ethics are probably not for you, no matter the possibilities.

THE REAL COST TO YOU

Wow, and probably wow again, even for the cheapest fast food franchise, you are going to have to be financially stable, not to mention have very deep pockets, to even think of taking one on successfully.

In the short term, it is easier to sell a franchise than to sell a fast-food outlet you have started yourself. The former has a nationwide name.

Let's face it, when you buy McDonald's or KFC, it's not because of a particular loyalty to your local fast food outlet, but certainly because of the name. Whilst the latter, your local fast-food outlet, is built by an entrepreneur who earns customer loyalty because you like his food and his way of doing things.

Although in the longer term, you are going to have a much bigger problem owning and running a franchise operation than you may like to consider. Not only are you going to have to pay a huge upfront fee, but from the very first dollar you earn, you are going to pay a percentage of it as a licensing charge.

Of course, all the while adhering to a very restrictive set of rules and practices following an intense training period or course. All of which are heavily regulated. If you get too many black marks for repeated breaches of company policy, or if there are discrepancies in the endless round of audits foisted on you, they will take away your franchise license.

That, of course, is the good part of the deal. Say, after 5 years, you are fed up with the whole thing, it has not returned anywhere near the profit, revenue, or returns you forecast, and you decide to sell. Well, exactly what are you going to sell?

You have no personal customer loyalty. You have no brand to sell, and you certainly don't own the name or intellectual property rights. All the pieces of the jigsaw that make any business irresistible to a potential buyer and a suitable reward for hard work and effort to the seller.

The whole point of it all is that if you don't make money when you are running a business, then you make that money back when you sell a business. The only problem is that in the franchise game, what you have achieved is only worth about a third of any other business, so that is the tragic reality of your gamble- a stark loss of 70%.

BUSINESS PARTNERS

It's not that you don't have friends, it's just that you are simply trying to survive in a dog-eat-dog world. You may have a perfect relationship with all those around you. Your personality is carrying you through the difficult times, and your management and negotiating skills are winning the day.

But beware: where there are people… there are problems!

I have personal experience of going into business with both friends and family. In both cases, a very bad idea. No matter whether the business is a roaring success or an abject failure, the strain will have repercussions on both relationships, which will take years – if ever – to recover.

I cannot stress enough that in business, you have very few friends. I also have a very painful experience with this. Do not get too close to those you deal with. Remember, your staff is not your friends. They are just your staff. Your suppliers are not your friends; no matter how much business you send their way, they are your suppliers.

There is an old saying, "Never mix business with pleasure." If you do choose this perilous route, make sure your attorney draws up a document between you and the person you are going into business with or borrowing money from, clearly stating terms, the length of the loan, payback conditions, and any other information that safeguards both parties.

Not for a moment should anyone try to undermine your potential relationship with your franchise partner, least of all me. But there are certain things that you should be aware of and get clear in your own mind before you start.

Running a successful fast-food franchise is akin to leading a small army. You are responsible for the front of house, the kitchen, deliveries, stock, suppliers, cleaners, and everything in between. You may employ a manager, but make no mistake about it, whether it is a restaurant you own or just one of many that you franchise, the buck stops with you.

It is an X-year commitment to a seven-day-a-week lifestyle. That realization may take a little time to sink in. Eventually, you become aware of the cost you are paying for the dream.

The Food Chain, So to Speak

Unfortunately, you may soon become aware that although you may have a good overall relationship with the franchise company, in the day-to-day running of the business, they are keeping a watchful eye on you.

Let's face it! You may have invested in the startup fund, undergone the training, and run the franchise day to day, but they are most certainly watching you.

In time, they hope to make money, perhaps a considerable sum from the fees that hang over your head. But they will call the shots!

Always check your costs when buying from the franchisor's suppliers, and even more so when buying supplies and products directly from the franchisor itself.

Look at the restrictions that the franchisor is imposing. One size does not always fit all. Does it suit your local market?

Are the franchise company's monitoring practices becoming intrusive into your own?

What if the franchisor itself goes out of business?

What if the very nature of the franchising game restricts your own personal growth, and of course, your own ideas of running what is essentially your business, after all?

As I said before, you will get back far less from selling an investment than from running it. It is a sad but true realization. Hopefully, in the successful years you have run the franchise, you will have offset your losses.

If you decide to sell, you may be bidding against your own franchiser, even if you don't know it.

A Note Regarding Contracts

Just to make sure you have understood everything that has gone before, I want to be sure you know what you are doing. Before signing anything, make sure you have all the basic and relevant information you may need.

It is a cardinal sin not to read, understand, or ask questions about the disclosure document. Do not for one second think that you can get away with not understanding, or having an inaccurate or incomplete interpretation of the franchise agreement and other legal documents to be signed. For goodness sake, there is no excuse for not seeking sound legal advice. You are a complete fool for not having enough working capital. You will soon go out of business for not analyzing your market in advance.

You will be selling yourself short by not meeting the franchisor's key management personnel at their headquarters and the field representative assigned to your territory before signing the agreement. I think, or at least hope, that by now you have the overall picture of your legal obligations to both you and the franchisor.

"Great achievement is usually born of great sacrifice and is never the result of selfishness."

Napoleon Hill – US Self-Help author

THE FUTURE OF FRANCHISES

There comes a time when any market becomes saturated, and that is certainly true of the fast-food market. There is some wily individual, a chef and entrepreneur, locked away in their secret underground kitchen, concocting the next great food idea. There are probably thousands of people out there trying to come up with that idea. It is anyone's guess as to who will succeed.

As I said earlier, it is the holy grail of ideas if you get it right. I read somewhere earlier this year that the family that came up with the idea for the Wal-Mart chain makes an average of $500K in profit per day.

GLOBAL INFLUENCE

China is a vast and as-yet-untapped market for the concept of globalization. Consider that the whole fast-food idea has grown considerably, especially amongst the middle class. In a recent report, 41% of China's population eats fast food at least once a week, compared with 31% in the USA.

Not surprisingly, China is the home of Chinese food, but the young in China are very tired of it, as they grew up with few other choices. They now want to taste various flavors and textures that can only be found at Pizza Hut, McDonald's, and KFC, although other brands are catching on and catching up.

Only 40 years ago, showing an interest in anything Western, never mind eating it, would have seen you imprisoned or even executed. Now, the authorities have softened that stance as they slowly open the doors to ideas other than their own. Why? Because there is vast money-making potential in the fast-food market. If Chinese businessmen are interested in anything, it is making money and as much of it as they can.

On average, one new fast-food experience opens in Beijing every day. Fast food is seen as far more sophisticated and far cleaner than traditional Chinese street food. The setback is that Western tastes are leading to Western weights and an increasing obesity problem, just like those they are trying to emulate.

So, if you are an entrepreneur who speaks Chinese, is unfazed by heaps of bureaucratic intervention, but who sees the potential in a market that is ripe for exploitation, take your fast food idea and see how it all may, or may not, develop.

REACHING A BROADER SCOPE

The thing to contemplate is how to make your fast-food idea global. How can you make that food item as universally appealing as you can possibly make it? Perhaps your big idea is chocolate grasshoppers, or crunchy cockroaches dipped in something or other and appearing on sticks. We have had 150 years of the conventional. What about another 150 years of the unconventional?

Perhaps the next big thing in plant-based recipes. Think of plant combinations of flavors, tastes, and textures that we can only dream about at the moment. That is going to take time and innovation of someone else's making.

Nothing in life is static. Willie Nelson wrote a song a number of years ago called "Still is Still Moving to Me," an analogy, of course. He likens a duck, swimming on the surface of the water, to serine, yet, underwater, their little webbed feet are working like mad just to keep them afloat.

It's a bit like people to be in someone else's brain. For even if you think you are in a state of stasis, you are not. You are still moving forward with your dreams, no matter your age you are. The only time you should stop dreaming is when you are dead.

NON-FOOD FRANCHISES

All in all, there is money in anything if you make the right choice. That is why the non-food market has exploded over the past few years. Surfing the internet, you can find an amazing range of choices available. I have looked at a few of them. It is just another option, and you should always keep them open.

Fast food is not the be-all and end-all of the franchise market. Should you really be at the beginning and wish to start a franchise, any franchise, but have no particular order, have a look below.

FIT4MOM

As a US operation, this company helps moms to get into shape and stay in shape after the baby is born, like Stroller Strides. They then develop a system to stay fit for life. A rather ingenious strategy to catch a mackerel: it is like McDonald's strategy of getting kids connected and then allowing them to grow with the organization.

In most cases, you must find your own venues, such as a school hall or a local community centre, but you then operate under the franchise brand name. It is your business, run at your pace to suit you, with all the help you need to make it a success.

The franchise fee ranges from $5,495 to $10,495, with an overall initial investment ranging from $6,205 to $24,285.

Stratus Building Solutions

This company is certainly looking to the future from day one of your involvement with them. They are an environmentally conscious franchisee with a strong emphasis on natural solutions to everyday cleaning problems.

Aimed at restaurants, schools, offices, and shopping malls, they are more than just a cleaning company. They are a cleaning company for tomorrow. They set up shop in 2006 and have grown substantially since then, as their no-frills, no-gimmicks service has caught on. They now run more than 1000 units.

Unlike many fast-food franchises, they seem eager to help investors get into the game. Even those with $5000 in cash have a chance of being accepted, and as they are very hands-on, offering financing options to help with the initial franchise fee, equipment, inventory, and other startup costs you may not have thought about. This company is worth a look if you are not convinced about the viability of a fast-food franchise.

The franchise fee is $2,700 to $100,000, with an initial investment of $3,450 to $100,000. You will need a net worth of at least $ 5,000 to $10,000 and a cash requirement of $2,000 to $20,000.

SUPERGLASS WINDSHIELD REPAIR

For all the car enthusiasts, within a very short training period, you could be part of the number one windshield repair franchise in the world.

Having recently been introduced into the UK, complementing some 400 other franchises around the globe, it offers a mobile solution to cracked and chipped windshield repair. Basically, it's an at-home business; they offer a fully equipped van, so you go to customers, not the other way around.

Whilst encouraging growth in the localized marketplace, they are very keen on rapid expansion and help drive their franchise owners into the large-volume marketplace.

The franchise fee is $5,000 to $17,500 with an investment of $18,685 to $84,205. Your personal investment is $15,000, with a minimum net worth of $15,000 cash requirement.

Dream Vacations

So far, on this list, we have had exercising moms, janitorial supplies, and windshield repair. How about running your own travel agency?

A low-cost franchise that offers, at least initially, another work-from-home option. The company is very smart, offering low-cost trips to the actual destination the franchise is selling, so that you, the franchisee, have first-hand knowledge of the region.

The franchise owner has won numerous travel-related awards. Their aim is to steer their franchise owners down the same path with a comprehensive training program and expert guidance in a very competitive market.

The franchise fee ranges from $495 to $9,800, with an initial investment ranging from $3,245 to $21,850.

So, there we have it, just four examples of the lower end of the market. There are literally hundreds of opportunities out there, covering just about any avenue you could wish to pursue, other than the fast-food option.

But look, I am totally fed up with giving you ideas! Go get some of your own! Think up the recipe, cook it, imagine a killer logo, and put together the marketing strategy to live your own dream!

"Fast food is both evil and genius. Because of it, we can feed many people fairly decently at a price. However, all the artificial Flavors and artificial ingredients in some of their products are unacceptable. And it's designed so you can eat fast and get back to work more quickly. Not good."

Eric Ripert - French chef, author, and TV personality

CONCLUSION

So, there we have it. Two choices to be made, two roads to be traveled. As you cannot serve two masters, it is also impossible to be a success in both fields at once. Never mind if you have the investment money or not.

If you look at it rationally, you will not remotely consider going into a franchise situation unless you have been involved in one from the outset or been an entrepreneur who has set up a fast food business and knows how to successfully run one. It stands to reason that if you have not succeeded at one before, attempting the other will probably end in tears.

Regardless of the simple practicalities of what you are doing, you cannot successfully do one unless you have done the other. If you are a genius who has all the bases ticked, then disregard this information. The experience of being a solo fast-food entrepreneur will be a foundation for taking the next step, should you wish, toward running a franchise.

As I mentioned earlier, everything you do in any business is simply a learning curve - a learning experience from one step to the next. Be sure you have mastered all the intricacies of the former before you ever attempt to do the latter.

No matter the path you take, I can only hope that the choice is right for you and that you succeed in whatever you choose to do.

Thank you so much for reading this book. If nothing else, I hope I have inspired you to keep going and pave your own way in this crazy world of fast food.

Would you do me a favor? Would you please leave me an online review on the platform where you purchased this book? I plan on personally reading every comment, and I welcome your feedback.

"A man must be big enough to admit his mistakes, smart enough to profit from them, and strong enough to correct them."

John C Maxwell – American, author, speaker, and pastor

BIBLIOGRAPHY

Below is a list of many of the websites I have consulted while writing this book. There are just too many resources to list in full, but there are many options out there for you to find.

The internet is a wonderful tool if used properly. It allows you to view, take notes, and make early decisions with very little effort, without leaving the comfort of either your desk or your armchair. Some are certainly more helpful than others, so be circumspect and weigh all your options. The more you look, the more you will learn!

With regards to books, try reading anything about any business you can get your hands on, not just the fast food industry. Read about companies like Virgin, Disney, IBM, Apple, etc. The list could go on forever, but they give you a good idea of how the big players in their particular fields did it.

I would also recommend the business books from Scribe Media, a US company, which specializes in telling the stories of success from all walks of business life.

Although the personal experiences in this book are my own, and the prose flows from my brain to my fingers and hence to my computer keyboard, I still need to use the services of the research sources as below. The many websites are listed in no particular order.

https://www.thebalancesmb.com/most-popular-food-franchises-and-how-much-they-cost-1350254

https://www.azquotes.com/search_results.html?query=fast+food+restaurants

https://www.barilla.com/en-gb/product-results/pasta/shape/long?sort=alpha

https://www.delish.com/food/g1549/snack-food-history/

https://theculturetrip.com/europe/germany/articles/a-brief-history-of-the-hamburger-2/https://www.entrepreneur.com/slideshow/308049https://www.startupdonut.co.uk/business-premises/commercial-premises/how-i-found-my-premises

https://www.lawdepot.co.uk/contracts/business-plan/?loc=GB&pid=msnppc-buspln_gb-https://www.goingbeyondwealth.com/your-moneys-worth-what-you-are-paying-for-in-a-franchise/businessplan_sl1-msnkey_a%20business%20plan&utm_source

https://www.mcdonalds.com/gb/en-gb/franchising.html

https://fitsmallbusiness.com/buying-vs-leasing-commercial-real-estate/

https://www.bpiauctions.com/auctions/catering/?msclkid=2a12d1e93d9416ef8cd78c0eb1e0c0be&utm_source=bing&utm_medium=cpc&utm_c

https://www.shopkeep.com/business-types/quick-service-restaurant-pos

https://www.foodstandards.gov.scot/business-and-industry/advice-for-new-businesses

https://www.thebalancesmb.com/business-startup-steps-to-do-first-3974584

https://www.wahm.com/articles/when-do-you-need-a-business-license.html

https://www.venturejapan.com/doing-business-in-japan/secrets-of-japanese-business-culture/

https://www.healthline.com/health/bacteria

https://www.magnifymoney.com/blog/personal-loans/getting-loans-from...

https://www.pointfranchise.co.uk/?gclid=EAIaIQobChMI47a3m-5gIViPhRCh0AsQN4EAAYAiAAEgKWs PDBwE

https://www.thebalancesmb.com/before-you-go-into-business-with-family-or-friends-397525

https://www.wendys.com/north-american-franchising-general-information#requirements

https://www.jerseymikes.com/franchise/investment

https://www.franchisehelp.com/franchises/krispy-kreme/